LISTEN OUT

International perspectives on
music education

Edited by
Chris Harrison
and
Sarah Hennessy

The authors of all chapters have been most generous in contributing to this book and we are very grateful to them. We are very happy to acknowledge the generous support of Rockschool for this publication, which is part of the work of NAME in supporting high-quality music education for all.

Generously supported by

ISBN 978-0-9566545-2-6

Editors: Chris Harrison and Sarah Hennessy
Cover design by Ad-lib Design Partnership Ltd, Worcester

© Copyright 2012 by the National Association of Music Educators
Registered charity number 1124612
A company limited by guarantee and registered
in England and Wales, number 6370539
Registered office: Slater Johnstone, 3 Thimble Lane,
Knowle, Solihull, West Midlands B93 0LY

Copyright of each chapter remains with the authors

CONTENTS

Foreword 5

Notes on the contributors 6

Introduction 9

Section 1: Student exchanges

Crossing borders, closing gaps — in favour of European
student exchanges in music education *Johanne Schröder* 14

Becoming a music teacher: a comparison between
Sweden and England *Joakim Nygren* 20

The international student forum: a supportive way to develop
the professional profile of future music teachers
Branka Rotar Pance and Gerhard Sammer 26

Section 2: Perspectives on teaching and learning

It's better in the Bahamas *Daniel Knight* 38

Teaching music in different cultural contexts:
Japan and England *Tomoko Ogusu* 47

'It's Revolutionary!': a case of
interdisciplinarity in music education *Eric Shieh* 56

Becoming a metropolitan music learner *Sinae Wu* 65

Young people's experiences of learning music in
other countries *James Garnett* 74

Section 3: International collaborations

'Now I dare to sing a song with the children, even with the
elder children.' Experiences of students and teacher educators
at the International Summer School in Educating Music Teachers
Sarah Hennessy, Ellen de Vugt and Michele Biasutti 78

Facilitation as leadership: empowering individuals within the
collective: a Soundcastle International Exchange in São Paulo, Brazil
Rachael Perrin, Jennifer Parkinson, Gail Macleod and Hannah Dunster...............86

Building international collaborative networks through creative
professional practice *Pamela Burnard*..95

Section 4: International initiatives

Sistema: where academic, educational, musical, personal and
social development all meet *Richard J. Hallam* 104

Achieving through diversity: music competitions and their role
in music education across Europe *Claire Goddard* 116

From Seoul to Bonn: a journey through international and
European music education policies *Simone Dudt*..126

Appendix

Useful websites and further reading 140

Foreword

Music might be 'the universal language of mankind' as Longfellow claimed, but that is not to say that the language of music is learned in the same way around the world. Far from it. Each of the chapters in this book unveils disparities of philosophy and practice compared with what we take for granted at home (wherever that is for you). Whether you dip into the book or read it continuously, the insights provided by successive chapters into the variety of attitudes and techniques, repertoire and institutions, will shine a new light on what is familiar from your own practice.

At a time of rapid change in music education, it is important both to value what we have, and to become aware of new possibilities. This book helps us to do both, making us more aware of what it is that we do and the assumptions that we make. In responding to rapid change, it is important not to become inward-looking and to hang on to what we are familiar with. This book will help us to turn our gaze outwards — to listen out for other ways of teaching music. This is not so that we can simply transplant them from one country into another; but so that our horizons widen, and we begin to see what we know as one of a number of possible approaches.

I am very grateful to the contributors to this book for sharing their experiences of working in different countries and their insights into the different cultures of music education. Some are members of NAME, some of sister organizations; but all have given generously of their time to prompt us to listen out. I am also grateful to the editors for their dedication and expertise in shaping the book. Finally, on behalf of all the Directors and Members of NAME, I would like to thank Rockschool, whose generous sponsorship means that this wealth of experience comes at an affordable price.

James Garnett
Chair, National Association of Music Educators
2011–2012

Notes on the contributors

Michele Biasutti PhD is an associate professor at Padova University, where he conducts research in psychology of music and music education. Research topics include cognitive processes in composition and improvisation, online music learning and the education of music teachers. He is scientific director of several research projects, he has published in international peer-reviewed journals and is author of seven books. He is currently President of the Italian Society for Music Education (SIEM)

Pamela Burnard is Reader in Education at the University of Cambridge, UK, where she manages Higher Degree courses in Arts, Creativity, Education and Culture (ACEC) and Educational Research. She is internationally known for her work in the areas of creative learning and teaching and musical creativities in professional, industry and educational practice.

Ellen de Vugt began her career as a music teacher and music co-ordinator in primary education and is currently working as a lecturer at the School of Education (primary education, music, arts and culture education) at Rotterdam University. She has been a board member of the national network for music teachers at teacher-training schools in the Netherlands.

Simone Dudt studied cultural sciences in Hildesheim, Germany, and Marseille, France, focusing on Fine Arts and Music. She worked for the educational programmes of several museums and music schools and as an academic assistant at the University of Hildesheim. She has been working for the European Music Council since 2004, where she co-ordinated the EU-funded 'ExTra! Exchange Traditions' project. Simone is executive editor of the EMC's 'Sounds in Europe' magazine. In 2010, she was elected to the Board of Culture Action Europe. Currently, she is Secretary General of the European Music Council.

Claire Goddard is Secretary General of EMCY (European Union of Music Competitions for Youth) and a Board Member of the European Music Council. She is active in the education and youth work of the European and International Music Councils and recently initiated and led two successful EU-funded projects focusing on international youth policy and participation. Claire grew up in Surrey where she took full advantage of the possibilities offered by the County Music Service, studied European Languages and Cultures at the University of Manchester (with an AHRC research scholarship) and is currently based in Munich, Germany.

Richard Hallam MBE has been a professional musician, teacher, curriculum advisor, inspector, head of music service and conductor. His national involvement in UK music education spans 18 years including being Chair of NAME, ISM Music Education Section Warden, member of the MEC executive and on numerous charitable, government and curriculum advisory bodies. He chaired the Music Manifesto steering committee, assisted with the Henley Review of Music Education and was the DfE's consultant for the National Plan for Music Education. He is currently a Director of In Harmony Sistema England, ISM President elect and a freelance music education consultant.

Chris Harrison is a music education consultant whose recent work includes teaching on ITE courses at London Metropolitan and Greenwich Universities, running courses for teachers and young musicians, and writing educational materials. A former teacher and local authority music adviser, he was Chair of NAME in 2006–7 and is currently Managing Editor (Publications) for the association. His musical tastes are wide-ranging and he performs with a number of groups and ensembles. He is particularly interested in the role of improvisation in learning music and in developing musical activities in the community at large.

Sarah Hennessy is Senior Lecturer in Music Education at the University of Exeter where she leads the primary music specialist PGCE course. She is also director of the Masters programme and supervises doctoral students. Her interests are focused on primary teacher education for both specialists and generalists; creative approaches in teaching and learning, and the work of arts professionals in education. She is founding editor of the journal Music Education Research and director of the international conference RIME held every two years. She is a past chair of NAME and EAS, and is now a board member of ISME.

Daniel Knight was born in Islington but grew up in Hampshire and Stevenage where he was an active member of the Stevenage Youth Orchestra and Choir and Hertfordshire County Music School. A pianist and tuba player, he attended Trinity College of Music in 1977. After gaining his PGCE at Bretton Hall, he taught in Tufnell Park for a year for the ILEA. Since then he has taught music in the Bahamas, Thailand, South Korea and Hong Kong. He gained his doctorate in education from the University of Sheffield in 2008 and currently lives and works in Hong Kong.

Joakim Nygren is a singer, songwriter, and musician from the south of Sweden. After his military service he worked for two years in a factory before enrolling as a student at the music academy in Malmö, Sweden. In the autumn of 2009 he began his training to become a music teacher. During summer 2010 he went to Spain to learn Spanish, and in autumn 2011 he took part in an Erasmus exchange programme, attending part of the secondary PGCE Music course at the University of Greenwich. He is now completing his studies in Sweden.

Tomoko Ogusu qualified as a music teacher in Japan, where her Masters degree included a study visit to the USA. After teaching in both state and private schools in Japan, she came to England in 2010 to study on a PGCE secondary music course at the University of Reading. She currently works as a music teacher in Bracknell and teaches Japanese at a Saturday school in London.

Branka Rotar Pance PhD is Assistant Professor and Head of the Department of Music Education at the Academy of Music (University of Ljubljana). She is a member of the board of the European Association of Music in Schools (EAS) and editor of the journal *Glasbeno- pedagoški zbornik Akademije za glasbo v Ljubljani.* Research areas include music education, lifelong learning of music teachers, arts and cultural education at school and the history of Slovenian music pedagogy.

Gerhard Sammer PhD is Professor of Music Education and Dean of Studies at the University for Music in Würzburg (Germany). He is Vice-president of the European Association of Music in Schools (EAS). He undertakes freelance work as conductor and is artistic director of the Tyrolean Chamber Orchestra *InnStrumenti*. Research areas include empirical research in music education, the methodology of music teaching, music-making and new media in the classroom, and music teacher training.

Johanne Schröder was born in 1986 and lives in Cologne, Germany. She was educated at Cologne University and at the Hochschule für Musik und Tanz. In 2009, she received a scholarship from the educational exchange programme of the Kultusministerkonferenz (the German conference of cultural ministers) to work as a German language assistant in the United Kingdom. She is currently a prospective trainee teacher and also works in socio-cultural music projects and for the music education office of the WDR orchestras in Cologne.

Eric Shieh currently teaches Music at the Metropolitan Expeditionary Learning School, 'A School for a Sustainable City,' in New York City. He is a former curriculum policy strategist for the New York City Department of Education, and his work in music education includes seven years building music programmes in prisons across the United States. His research interests centre on radical pedagogies and curricular change, with recent articles addressing social justice and music education, youth culture, and the politics of professional associations in curriculum reform. Eric holds an Ed.M. in Curriculum and Teaching from Teachers College, Columbia University in New York.

Soundcastle is a London-based arts collective comprising four professional musicians: Hannah Dunster (flute), Gail MacLeod (recorder), Jenni Parkinson (marimba) and Rachael Perrin (clarinet). Their mission is to explore exciting and inspiring approaches to music-making, to promote music as an individual and collective voice, to develop projects that are sustainable and to maintain an ongoing community of artists and creative participants. They devise and lead site-specific, collaborative and cross-arts work, lead and facilitate creative music projects in community settings and form dynamic new music ensembles. Alongside this they curate artistic events, research artistic practice and provide professional development opportunities for musicians and leaders.

Sinae Wu is a PhD research student at the Institute of Education, University of London. She was born in Seoul, Korea. After studying at the National Traditional Music High School she entered Seoul City University, where she studied music theory, composition and piano. She then moved to Berlin and spent a decade studying harpsichord (Berlin University of Arts) and musicology (Berlin Institute for Technology). She came to England and attained Qualified Teacher Status at London Metropolitan University in 2011. Her MA dissertation at the Institute of Education (2012) dealt with issues of musical identity among students from multicultural backgrounds.

Introduction

The teaching profession is inevitably focused on the context in which it practises, and within music education those who work in the state school sector are perhaps the most focused. Increasing demand and accountability make it difficult to stick one's head over the parapet to see what is happening in a neighbouring school let alone a neighbouring country. Certain traditions in instrumental teaching, on the other hand, can make it relatively easy to travel and relate to practices at an international level. For students and teachers at advanced levels in the classical and jazz worlds, for instance, there are opportunities to study almost anywhere in the world and an international background is greatly respected.

Teachers in schools are in a very different situation — concerned with the social context in which pupils live and learn, engaging with the musical culture of the locality, and working within institutions in which music is only a small part of the whole. Everything that happens in a school is a reflection of its history, its current environment and the national agenda. It is no surprise, then, that it is in the interests of school-based teachers, those that train them and those that rely on them for at least part of their work, to become very knowledgeable about and skilled in negotiating this environment. This leaves little time and energy to learn much about anywhere else, sometimes leading to teachers feeling isolated and starved of support and new ideas — something that Ofsted commented on in its most recent report (2012).

The constraints of the training regime in England make it nigh on impossible for students to do placements outside the country (not even in Wales) and mean that new teachers may develop a narrow view of what music education can be. For experienced teachers it is equally difficult as there is almost no allowance for study trips. As mentioned later, exchanges and participation in funded projects seem to be the most fruitful path. Getting involved in a project not only generates better knowledge and appreciation of music education internationally but, of course, facilitates contact with professionals in other countries. These contacts often develop beyond the initial impetus and may lead to further collaborations — student teacher visits; pupils meeting online to share their music-making, generating new projects. The EU Comenius programme (see appendix) is designed to promote and facilitate such activity, and fund it.

Of course some music teachers and music education practitioners, at different stages of their development, do make the leap, whether a one-way or a return journey, and it is clear that there are real benefits from learning about how music education is conceptualized and practised in other countries. Getting involved in international networks can help us not only to learn about different approaches to music education, but also to identify what we have in common.

In Europe, the meNet project (http://menet.mdw.ac.at/menetsite/english/) has gathered information about music education in 19 European countries, while the EU also hosts a huge amount of statistical and descriptive data on education systems in Europe (http://eacea.ec.europa.eu/education/eurydice/index_en.php), including interesting data on arts education. From these and other sources, we can see that the vast majority of countries include music in their school curriculum and train specialist teachers for certain age phases. A common feature, and one of some concern, is that many countries, even those with well-established music education and no great shortage of resources, have patchy primary music provision with the usual muddle of inadequate generalist training and insufficient numbers of specialists. It is also worth noting that the majority of countries in Europe have a system of state funded or subsidized music schools for children, taking place out of normal school hours. Access varies but their presence may have the effect of weakening the status of music in the school curriculum, bringing a potential divide in the profession so that in some countries it is more prestigious to work in the specialist music schools. Another important difference with the UK is that instrumental teachers are almost always trained with a degree-level qualification, like school teachers. Readers will recognize what a difference this makes to the professional community.

The contributors to this book give their own accounts of working in different countries or getting involved in international projects. We begin in **Section 1** with some accounts of student exchanges. Johanne Schröder, a student teacher from Cologne, describes her experiences working in an Oxfordshire primary school. She offers some interesting comparisons between practices in Germany and the UK, and is an enthusiastic advocate of the benefits of student exchanges. Joakim Nygren, from Malmo, Sweden, spent three months at Greenwich University on an Erasmus programme, which included two school placements. He describes differences between schools and the teacher-training systems in the two countries. Finally, Branka Rotar Pance and Gerhard Sammer give us a history of the international EAS Student Forum and an insight into the issues that concern students across a range of different European countries.

Section 2 focuses on different experiences of teaching and learning. Daniel Knight has worked in Sudan, the Bahamas, Thailand, South Korea and Hong Kong. He describes a fascinating journey through different cultures and offers some general reflections on working abroad. Tomoko Ogusu became interested in music education outside of Japan while a student in Tokyo. She is now working as a teacher in England and her chapter offers some detailed comparisons between the curricula of the two countries. Eric Shieh describes an innovative approach to teaching in a New York school and offers a passionate argument in favour of cross-curricular teaching. Sinae Wu grew up in Korea and subsequently studied in Germany and the UK. She reflects on different approaches to teaching and learning on her journey as a 'metropolitan music learner'. We conclude this section with some extracts from interviews with students now living in England who began their schooling in another country. They give us a brief but nonetheless welcome sense of the learner's point of view.

Section 3 looks at international collaborations and begins with an account of an International Summer School which took place in Padua in three consecutive years (2010–12). As well as describing the content of the workshop programme, the chapter offers reflections from students and staff on the effectiveness and the benefits of this initiative. Members of Soundcastle, a London-based arts collective, describe their experience of working in Brazil, including reflections on how their own method of working was received and what they have learnt from others, including a timely encounter with the idea of *musica com linguagem* ('music as language'). Lastly, Pam Burnard reflects on the benefits of being involved with other practitioners in building and developing international collaborative networks, a process she describes as 'truly magical'.

In **Section 4**, we offer descriptions of some international initiatives. Richard Hallam outlines the essential characteristics of *El Sistema* and describes how the programme, in various forms, has been taken up in different countries all over the world. Claire Goddard's chapter shows us that music competitions in Europe have a different emphasis and play a different role from those in England. Finally, Simone Dudt gives us an overall context by providing a helpful summary of international and European policies including the Seoul Agenda and the Bonn Declaration.

Of course, funding for international projects is always an issue, and lack of knowledge about what funding is available is a major deterrent even to thinking about the possibilities. Our appendix offers details of useful websites and further reading for those who are stimulated by the experiences described in the book to get involved in international activities. If readers know of other examples, a short report for the NAME Magazine would be very useful.

A great truism is that we learn more about our own practice by observing that of others. In an uncertain world it becomes imperative that we test what we value, and a useful, interesting and positive way to do this is to visit and interact with teachers in other circumstances — and other cultures and countries.

Some 50 years ago, the Schools Music Association published the results of a worldwide survey of music education (SMA, 1964). In his foreword, the secretary of the association wrote:

> It becomes increasingly important that countries should keep each other informed of what each other is doing in this field, as progress can thereby be accelerated when all interested persons are aware of what is being done in countries other than their own.

We hope that the experiences and reflections of the contributors to this book will encourage readers to explore new possibilities and help us all to reflect on and develop our own practice.

Chris Harrison
Sarah Hennessy

References

Ofsted (2012) *Music in schools: wider still, and wider. Quality and inequality in music education 2008–11.* London: Ofsted

SMA (1964) *Music in Schools: a world survey.* London: Schoolmaster Publishing

Section 1

Student exchanges

Crossing borders, closing gaps — in favour of European student exchanges in music education

Johanne Schröder

> „Die beste Bildung findet ein gescheiter Mensch auf Reisen."
> The best education for a clever person is found in travel.
> J.W. von Goethe (1749–1832), *Wilhelm Meisters Lehrjahre*

As a student of English and music from Cologne, Germany, I spent nine months on a scholarship of the educational exchange programme of the *Kultusministerkonferenz*, the German conference of cultural ministers, working as an assistant teacher at a secondary school in Oxfordshire from September 2009. The first week at my school in England left me enthusiastic: I was working at an all-day, comprehensive, inclusive school. Only a very small number of German schools managed to combine these three features at that time and the transition towards *Eine Schule für Alle*[1] whereby inclusive comprehensive schools would replace the traditionally highly selective three-tier school system, was still controversially debated at universities and in the media. Thus, I embraced a variety of new impressions and ideas, while being most curious about the ways music education worked in this context inside and outside the school. Naturally, I found myself constantly confronted with the differences and similarities between my experiences at home and abroad. This article is a field report rather than a comparative approach to two educational systems, as it is highly subjective and focused on the everyday experience of my exchange year. However, some of the concepts I learned led me to consider how music education in German schools could benefit from British ideas and which developments in Germany could radiate back across the Channel. Negotiating subjective impressions and theoretical information is thereby a process, which is still ongoing, two years after my gap year. But being aware of the diversity of international music education concepts, school systems, socio-political structures and the difficulties of intercultural communication should not keep us from being simply inspired by new ideas. Thus, my aim is to advocate exchanges and visiting programmes for students of music education in addition to the research in comparative music education and to academic exchanges, which have already gained ground at European universities. Having the chance to visit other countries and experience how young people learn music while still being a student yourself is a great way of preparing to be a music teacher in a globally-orientated society.

I was in the penultimate year of my studies when I went abroad, hoping to improve my English, to experience everyday life at a British school and to travel around England, Scotland and Ireland, before returning for my final exams in Germany. I had just passed my examinations in performance-orientated subjects at the *Musikhochschule*[2] in Cologne where I was studying and thus had spent almost a year practising very hard. This is because the final exams of the programme of music education which I studied at the *Musikhochschule* are divided into artistically-orientated exams in the third year of study (for instance in the major and minor instrument, in piano and conducting) and academically-orientated exams in the fourth and fifth year (such as musicology, educational science and music pedagogy). So when I came over to England, I was happy to find some distraction by 'only' teaching German as a foreign language. However, while working primarily as a language assistant, I soon found myself observing and assisting in music lessons, supervising a student jazz band once a week, judging the 'singer of the year' competition and working with the school's chamber choir, where we rehearsed a choral piece by Mendelssohn. I was also singing in a choir in Oxford and through this I took part in a music education project for comprehensive school students in Oxfordshire organized in co-operation with the Royal Philharmonic Orchestra. In addition to what I learned in the Modern Foreign Languages classroom, I found this an enriching experience of music teaching in a context completely different from that which I was from.

Aspects of the English school system, which might appear to be self-evident to British people, were surprisingly new for me. I was well aware that in contrast to the majority of German schools, British schools were organized full-time, but now I saw the effect of this policy on the lives of teachers and students: for both groups, school was a place not only to 'learn' but also to 'live', as everybody spent a large part of the week in school. This particular school, however, managed superbly to allow the students room for recreation and extra-curricular activities and thus made efficient use of the seven hours a day that everyone, on average, spent at school. Another striking difference was the school's extensive equipment with ICT and musical facilities. Students were offered a wide range of possibilities not only to experience their 'formal' music education in school, but also to enhance this on an informal level. In the detached building of the music department, students were given the opportunity to practise a range of available instruments or meet for band rehearsals during breaks and after school. Sixth form students were allowed to work on their arrangements and compositions at the computers situated in the back of the class, even when younger year groups were in the room. Small soundproof practice rooms provided space for everyone to experiment as well as for students to extend their learning — regardless of whether the students' families were able to afford their own instruments. Moreover, a co-operation with the local music school involved regular music lessons in the rooms of the music department. Students attending these music lessons were allowed to leave their classrooms — a remarkable thing in my experience, which demonstrates how highly music education is valued among other teachers and within the whole school.

In Germany, many schools still struggle to accomplish the requirements of full-time education within the country's very diverse and fragmented educational landscape, as the requirement to create more *Ganztagsschulen,* schools which provide all-day education, only arose after the controversial results of the PISA study in 2000 (the OECD Programme for International Student Assessment). Even now, more than a decade later, the policy still faces substantial resistance. Moreover, education in schools is not organized nationally, but by the 16 federal states, resulting in a diversity of school policies and curricula. Governmental initiatives similar to the English National Plan for Music Education (NPME) or the National Curriculum do not exist. This is also why public investment in education varies considerably across the country. And, considering the comparatively low expenditure of 4.59 % of the GDP for schools and education in Germany (Malmberg & Sammler, 2010), compared to 5.5 % in the UK[3], it is not surprising that we find more blackboards and classroom percussion instruments in music classrooms than interactive whiteboards, new computers and band instruments. Furthermore, schools and music schools have only recently become less anxious about developing collaborative concepts to establish full-time education, for instance through trust initiatives like *Jedem Kind ein Instrument*, which started in 2007 in the Ruhr area. From my experience in England, I was encouraged to believe that music schools might see an opportunity rather than a threat in all-day education, insofar as it offers new possibilities for co-operation and communal engagement (see also Ritter, 2010).

Another impressive experience for me was a Royal Philharmonic Orchestra Resound education project in Oxford. Even though more and more orchestras in Germany have started to run outreach education projects, this whole field of educational work is comparatively new. It was only in 2004 that the documentary film *Rhythm is it!* (Grube & Sánchez-Lanch, 2004) about the Berlin Philharmonic's community dance project staging Stravinsky's *Sacre du Printemps* became enormously popular in Germany and began to raise an awareness of the possibilities of educational work by professional orchestras. Since then, new professional positions, study programmes and further education courses have been created, which contributed a lot to establishing and consolidating music education projects among professional orchestras in Germany.

However, it was a completely new and inspiring experience for me to observe how such a project was realized and conducted in practice. I was especially impressed by the focus on composition and the productive character of the project, which brought a newly-composed Requiem to the stage in only one week. Instead of being designed to *explain* the music of the RPO, the project's aim was to get children to *create* their own music. The success of the final concert left me moved by a wonderful and artistic piece of music and impressed me with the idea of how much more can be 'taught' through not teaching at all.

Of course, being inspired by some of the conditions of music education in England and newly aware of 'untapped potentials' in the German educational system does not imply that there is such a thing as a hierarchy between the two. Rather, my impressions demonstrate how a change of perspective during an exchange year opens your eyes to particular aspects, which are different to what you knew before. I am convinced that positive aspects of music education in Germany might be more effectively depicted by music students from other European countries than by German students observing the system from within.

So what is it that could indeed 'radiate back' across the Channel? Which aspects of music education at German schools could be particularly interesting for other European countries? A great strength lies in the abundance of the music teacher training system in Germany. There exists a variety of specialized training programmes for aspiring music teachers for all the different types of schools. Subject pedagogy, methodology and educational science are combined with a strong focus on artistic training right from the start, especially at *Musikhochschulen*. This includes, for instance, training in conducting and piano-playing especially designed for the purposes of the classroom (with an emphasis on accompaniment, score reading and improvisation) lasting up to four years. Moreover, students are encouraged to take at least two different courses, which enables them to teach two different subjects later. In my case, I chose English as a foreign language, which I studied at Cologne University, and music for secondary school teaching at the *Musikhochschule* in Cologne. Constantly alternating between the two institutions and academic fields has been challenging, but also eye opening. Being trained to teach subjects as diverse as music and geography, a modern foreign language or Latin, sports or history makes teachers versatile and offers students an extensive *Bildung*[4]. Being trained in a broader range of subjects encourages students to develop creative ideas, including cross-curricular teaching methods and projects, for instance the possibilities of bilingual music teaching.

In her argument for the importance of comparative music education, Alexandra Kertz-Welzel (2007) points out how, in relation to music education in schools, similar issues are discussed across Europe: dealing with standards, multiculturalism, student behaviour and learning music outside the classroom. If we acknowledged the medium of our subject to be of a transcultural and hybrid nature, when do we start assuming the same for its pedagogy? I believe that exchange projects like 'Discoveries in music' (2005), organized by the *Hochschule für Musik und Theater Rostock*, the Socrates Intensive Programme 'School music in a European perspective' (2007) at the *Hochschule für Musik und Theater, Leipzig* and the annual student forum of the European Association for Music in Schools (EAMS) are breaking new ground. Universities and schools across Europe should be encouraged to run similar projects in order to establish and embed a culture of student exchanges, which allow experiences in academic discipline, performance and school practice in equal measure. My own experience of music teaching in England happened more or less as a by-product of being a language assistant, and I am convinced that much more scientifically-based observations and empirical analysis would be possible if exchanges in the future were professionally supervised and conducted by universities.

Current developments in the educational landscape in Germany are likely to result in essential features of school education, like the inclusion of children with special needs, all-day education and the rise of comprehensive and communal schools, becoming the new realities in which aspiring teachers will be operating in the coming years. There is evidence that old structures will be forced open and Germany might be gradually leaving its European *Sonderweg*[5]. As music education students and interns, we can look forward to a broader spectrum of professional practice, as music teaching will probably involve working with new technologies, more partnership projects within the communities and new teaching methods to encourage independent and co-operative learning.

During my years at university, some of these changes were already becoming visible. When I passed my *Abitur*[6] in 2005, I was a student at a *Gymnasium* in the north of Germany, where we had on average six lessons of 45 minutes a day, starting at 7:45 and ending at 13:05. My musical education was entirely financed by my parents and took place in a local musical school, which I attended once a week, and in the church choir, where I sang on Monday afternoons and Sunday mornings. Music lessons in school were rare and mostly dealt with the history of classical music in Germany. Today, this has changed. My old school now offers day-long education and has become a *Ganztagsschule* with a special focus on cultural education and community music and dance projects. There are more combined lessons, which break open the narrow confines of 45 minutes and increasingly encourage cross-curricular activities.

Personally, I am interested and enthusiastic about how these developments will continue in the future. To a great extent, this new interest in and enthusiasm for the changes was encouraged by what I learned abroad. A couple of years ago, when I started my studies, I probably would not have thought that these things were possible. In fact, I remember being anxious at the prospect of teaching in unfamiliar and constantly changing contexts and would then have taken the 'safe choice' of doing my teacher training at a traditional *Gymnasium*. But, returning to Cologne, I was encouraged to start a job in a community musical project at a newly-founded *Gemeinschaftsschule*[7] in a disadvantaged neighbourhood and to broaden my horizon of inclusive and intercultural music education. Today I hope that more students like me will experience other contexts of music education across Europe in a way that will similarly change their lives and perspectives on education.

References:

Grube, T & Sánchez-Lanch, E. (2004) *Rhythm is it!* Berlin: Boomtown Media.

Kertz-Welzel, A. (2007) „Community Music: Der internationale Diskurs über außerschulische Musikvermittlung" In: *Diskussion Musikpädagogik*. Hamburg: Junker-Verlag 33: 44–48.

Malmberg, I. & Sammler, G. (2010) „Musikunterricht in Europa. Einblicke in die Vielfalt der musikalischen Bildung." In: *mip journal*. Esslingen a. Neckar: Helbling-Verlag 27: 6–11.

Mattes, M. (2007) Tagungsbericht „The German Half-Day Model: A European Sonderweg? The ‚Time Politics' of Child Care, Pre-School and Elementary School Education in Post-War Europe. 01.03.2007–03.03.2007, Potsdam". In: H-Soz-u-Kult, 18.05.2007, <http://hsozkult.geschichte.hu-berlin.de/tagungsberichte/id=1569>. (accessed August 5th 2012).

Nuissl, E. (2012) *Bildung. Germany*. URL: www.eaea.org/index.php?k=15098 (August 5th 2012).

Ritter, B. (2010) *Musikalische Bildung in der Ganztagsschule*. URL: www.miz.org/fachbeitraege.html (June 19th 2012).

Reich, K. (2008) „Demokratie und Didaktik — oder warum Schulentwicklung und Inklusion nicht beliebig sein können." In: Ziemen, K. (Hg.): *Reflexive Didaktik. Annäherungen an eine Schule für alle*. Oberhausen (Athena) 2008.

Links:

Educational Exchange Programme of the German conference of cultural ministers: www.kmk-pad.org/

MeNet — Music education Network: www.menet.info

Programme for International Student Assessment: www.pisa.oecd.org

Jedem Kind ein Instrument: www.jedemkind.de/

Eine Schule für Alle: www.eine-schule-fuer-alle.info/

Socrates Intensive Programme 'School music in a European perspective': www.hmt-leipzig.de/index.php?Schoolmusic-in-a-European-Perspective

Discoveries in music: http://idw-online.de/pages/de/news?print=1&id=101115

EAS student forum: www.eas-music.org/activities/student-forum-sf/2011-gdansk-pl/report/

RPO education project: www.rpo.co.uk/colour_is_reborn.php

UK Education expenditure as a proportion of GDP: www.education.gov.uk/rsgateway/DB/TIM/m002002/index.shtml

Endnotes

1. Literally 'one school for all' — further information at www.eine-schule-fuer-alle.info/

2. *Musikhochschulen* are institutions developed from conservatoires to establish academic training in the arts and are equated to the scientific universities.

3. Figure from the Department for Education website, updated January 2008. www.education.gov.uk/rsgateway/DB/TIM/m002002/index.shtml (accessed May 2012)

4. The German concept of *Bildung* is not exactly translateable. According to Ekkehard Nuissl, for instance, *Bildung* not only implies the dimension of teaching but also that of learning (*sich bilden*), not only knowledge and skills, but also values, ethos, personality, authenticity and humanity. He also points out that 'the complexity of the term accounts for the fact that *Bildung* is seen as the appropriate expression for the totality of all teaching and learning related activities in Germany (. . .).' (Nuissl, 2012).

5. The term 'Sonderweg' means 'a unique way' and is used by educational scientists to critically refer to the historical path of German educational politics in comparison to other European countries (see Mattes, 2007). They argue, for instance, that the traditional German half-day model of education stands for a policy which differs fundamentally from other European countries. Kersten Reich (2008) moreover applies the term also to criticize the existence of *Förderschulen* in Germany — in contrast to a nationwide introduction of comprehensive schools which also include students with special needs. The 'German Sonderweg' in education, he argues, is characterized by the highly selective three-tier school system, the half-day policy, which still privileges traditional family models, the existence of separated *Förderschulen* for students with special needs and the teacher training system, which still emphasizes subject knowledge compared to psychological and pedagogical competencies.

6. *Abitur* is the term for the final examinations at German *Gymnasien* (grammar schools) and *Gesamtschulen* (comprehensive schools) after grade 12 or 13, which traditionally provide the general qualification for university entrance.

7. *Gemeinschaftsschule* (community school) stands for a new concept of schools, which has been introduced to Germany first in 2007 in Schleswig-Holstein. It is a type of comprehensive school, where students learn conjointly from year 1 to year 10 and is thus considered to be an 'alternative model' to the traditional school system in Germany.

Becoming a music teacher: a comparison between Sweden and England

Joakim Nygren

I am currently studying to become a music teacher in Sweden. So far I have done three out of a total of five and a half years. At the beginning of my third year I went on an Erasmus exchange for four months, to join the secondary PGCE course at the University of Greenwich. During these months I gained a lot of new knowledge and experience which I will try to describe in this chapter.

As the educational systems in Sweden and England are not very similar, it follows that there are quite a few differences between the two countries with regard to teacher education, including the nature of the school placement. I will reflect on these and on some other aspects of teaching in English schools.

Differences in the overall education system

You will be familiar with terms such as KS1 to KS3, GCSE, BTEC and A levels. As a Swedish person I had never heard of these words before I came to England. Furthermore, I did not know that English pupils begin school at the age of five, compared to age seven for Swedish pupils. To show the differences between our two countries' educational systems, I will start by briefly outlining what the Swedish system looks like.

In Sweden we have community schools, 'free schools' and very few private schools. Everyone is free to choose which school they want to go to, but people who live in the catchment area of a school have priority over those who live outside it. This leaves Swedish students with quite limited choices. English students, have many more options — community, grammar, academies, faith, and independent schools. In addition, these schools may be either single sex or mixed schools. The advantage of the English system is that a student can (in theory) choose a school environment where they feel at home and where other students share the same values. However, under the Swedish system, students have more opportunities to learn how to deal with and tolerate these different values.

With the exception of higher education, the whole educational system in Sweden is organized in three-year stages. Hence there is the low stage (students of age 7–9, years 1, 2, 3), the middle stage (age 10–12, years 4, 5, 6), the high stage (age 13–15, years 7, 8, 9), and finally the gymnasium (age 16–18, where the years are also called 1, 2, 3). At the age of 15, in year 9, Swedish students apply for a programme at a gymnasium.

When the students begin their programme, at the age of 16, they can study their own choice of subjects as well as the core subjects that everyone studies. The core subjects are Swedish, English, Maths, PE, Science, Religious Studies and Social Studies. By contrast, English students start focusing on specific subjects at the age of 14, when they take their GCSEs. Later, when starting their A levels, they focus on even fewer subjects. As I see it, English students receive a narrower education, and also have to make big choices about their education earlier in life. While the advantage of this is that you gain deeper knowledge in these few subjects, it means that you lose the breadth of study. I believe that a wider education is more beneficial in your everyday life than a narrow one.

Initial teacher education

To get into a music teacher programme in Sweden two things are necessary: you need to graduate from the gymnasium (or equivalent), and complete some tests at the music academy. These tests consist of both practical and theoretical musical tests, and one teaching test. In the teaching test the applicant leads a 10–15 minute lesson with up to eight fellow applicants acting as 'pupils'. The lesson must be prepared beforehand on a subject of the applicant's choice.

The applicant is assessed on his or her ability to show positive leadership and engage everyone in the lesson, as well as on imagination and creativity in the choice of material and how he or she is able to adapt the content to the situation. Upon passing these tests and being accepted into the music academy, between 4½ and 5½ years of education in pedagogy, different instruments, theory and many other subjects awaits. This is in contrast to England, where the PGCE is in fact a post-graduate course, and in order to be accepted you need an honours degree at 2:2 or above, preferably in music or a music-related subject, as well as GCSEs in mathematics and English above grade C. In short, you need a degree in music to become a music teacher.

In Sweden, students get the opportunity to learn a wide array of different instruments, as well as having singing lessons. Alongside this is the pedagogy, music history from different periods, a range of projects, music technology, choir (both as a singer and conductor), and teaching placements. All in all this might seem a heavy workload for the student, but at the same time the breadth of the education is invaluable for the future classroom teacher. Many of my cohort at Greenwich had completed an undergraduate course on their own instrument before attending the one-year PGCE course, which focuses on pedagogy, some music projects, and placements.

There are of course advantages and disadvantages with both systems. In Sweden, where the music is closely linked with both pedagogy and placement, the student learns what is needed for the classroom situation as a musician and can, by focusing on this, improve their skills with their instrumental teachers. In addition to their main instrument, a Swedish student has lessons on piano, guitar, drums, bass, singing, and maybe a further instrument of their own choice. They also have lessons in how to lead both a choir and an ensemble. The negative side of the Swedish educational system may be that the student has little chance to achieve a high level on their main instrument. In contrast, an English student may have achieved a very high level on their main instrument from their undergraduate studies, but does not have the opportunity to achieve the same breadth as a Swedish student.

This lack of breadth, however, is compensated in two different ways in England. The first is that, at Greenwich University, students are required to complete a subject enhancement form. Here the student reflects on what he or she needs to learn and sets up for him/herself short-, mid- and long-term goals. These goals are set together with both the teacher at the University and the mentor at the placement school. The goals can be of different types, for example to develop instrumental skills, to improve behaviour management in the classroom, or to read up on a specific musical tradition or genre. An equivalent of this does not exist in Swedish music teacher education. Secondly, the English student also has the opportunity to work alongside PGCE students from other subjects during their professional studies sessions, hence giving them more strategies for, for example, collaborating with other subjects. In contrast, Swedish students are completely separated from other students in other subjects, since all professional studies sessions take place only with music teacher students. This can of course also be beneficial for the Swedish student since the problems and questions dealt with in the Swedish professional studies sessions are dealt with in detail from the perspective of music teacher students.

School placements

During the one-year PGCE course, an English student undertakes 120 days of placement, whilst a Swedish student will only have around 70 days during their whole training programme. This is of course very valuable for the English student, since it is during the placement that you learn the most. It is also during your placement that you gain most experience about the job, the school you are at and, most importantly, the pupils. For me personally, during my time in England, it also meant gaining knowledge of different types of school that we do not have in Sweden, such as single-sex schools and grammar schools. I was lucky to experience both a girls' grammar school and a comprehensive school for boys during my time in England.

By law, single-sex schools are not allowed in Sweden as it is regarded as discrimination against gender. There might of course be certain classes in a Swedish school containing only boys or only girls, but this is not very common and would be the result of students' own subject choices rather than any restrictions on access. Therefore it was a tremendous experience and opportunity for me to be able to observe and teach at these kinds of schools during my placement. Based on my personal experience from both Sweden and England, I cannot say that I feel that either mixed schools or single-sex schools are better than the other. Some pupils do their homework, while some do not. Some pupils talk during class, while some do not. It seems to me that some teachers in both Sweden and England believe that a student's gender determines how well they can achieve in school, and also how they behave. I think that there is much more to it than just gender, and that single-sex schools have the same problems as mixed schools: bullying, talking in the classroom, and misbehaving. This occurs in all schools I have been in, both in Sweden and England. The only difference between Swedish and English classrooms on the matter of behaviour appears to be the authority given to the teacher. From what I have seen, a teacher in England seems to have more authority than Swedish teachers.

For me, the biggest difference between Sweden and England, when it comes to placements, is the QTS standards. The English student has a file where he or she keeps evidence to show that they have achieved these standards. Of course Sweden also has criteria for assessment, but the student teacher does not have to provide proof for these criteria. Instead, it is up to the subject teacher or mentor at the placement school to observe and decide if the student teacher achieves these criteria. When the placement is finished the Swedish mentor informs the University if the student passed or not. I really think that the English system is much better than the Swedish one. It makes the student aware of the criteria even more and helps them to reflect upon how to achieve them. Students in Sweden are less aware of the criteria, and are only informed about their progress if there is something that their mentor thinks they are lacking.

There are also significant differences in the way we approach lesson planning and evaluation. In England, the student teacher plans their lesson, and then their mentor looks through it and either approves it or asks for it to be revised. After teaching their lesson, feedback is given to the student by their observing mentor. The student teacher must then reflect upon their lesson and improve their lesson plan. This seems to me to be very thorough and ensures that the lessons really are improved. In Sweden this process is less strictly regulated. The student must of course plan lessons, and these plans must be approved by their mentor. However, the lesson plan does not need to be revised or improved unless it is really very unsatisfactory. The mentor also gives feedback after an observed lesson and maybe gives some suggestions to the student for the future.

I also find that English lessons are planned in so much more detail. In the PGCE course we were given forms for lesson planning. Learning objectives and learning outcomes were to be indicated, as well as cross-curricular links, an audit of NC key processes, inclusion, and personalized learning. Then, of course, there is also a detailed plan of the lesson itself. The lesson plans I have had to do so far in Sweden have not been as detailed as this. I feel that Swedish lesson plans lack the learning outcomes, personalized learning, and the cross-curricular links. I believe that we can learn a lot from the English way of planning lessons, but at the same time you need to be able to let go of the lesson plan if something occurs in the class that was not foreseen.

The placement school seems to be much more involved in England. When out on placements in Sweden, you have the subject teacher as your mentor. This is the person you send your planned lessons to, and you also have to send copies of these to your university teacher. The mentor observes you and once in every placement (we have four different placements) a teacher from the university will come to the school and observe you. In England, in addition to what we have in Sweden, there is also a named person at the school who informs all the student teachers about the school, and is available to talk to if anyone has any problems with their placement. The placement school also provides lectures or seminars in professional studies which student teachers can attend. These lectures and seminars are based on that particular school's actual practice, which is better than made up or outdated examples which the university might provide.

There has recently been a reform in the teacher education system in Sweden. This reform means that after examination by the University, the student has a status equivalent to the English newly qualified teacher (NQT). This signifies that a Swedish NQT is not a fully qualified teacher until he or she has been working as a teacher for a full year. After this year the NQT is allowed to apply for 'teacher identification' once the head teacher at the school has written a certificate of suitability. It is not until after the student has this identification that the NQT becomes a 'real teacher' and is allowed to grade his or her students. This induction period, and the recommendation from the head teacher, is quite similar to the English system, although there is one important difference: an English NQT only has one chance to pass and become a fully qualified teacher, while Swedish NQTs do not have any restrictions on how many chances they have to pass.

Other aspects of school life

When it comes to security at the schools, there is a really big difference. Almost anyone can walk into a school in Sweden without having to sign in or show any ID. I think that it is a good thing that the security level in England is as high as it is. A school needs to be able to provide a safe environment, for both students and staff. In my experience I would argue that not many Swedish schools can provide this.

The first time I visited a secondary school in England, I saw students wearing school uniform. This is something that we do not have in Sweden. Some research suggests that school uniforms can make schools safer, improve attendance, raise academic achievement, and help students concentrate. However, just comparing Sweden and England in the international PISA surveys[1], Swedish students achieve higher results than English students, and this without a school uniform. Moreover, the time spent on telling the students to wear their uniform correctly would surely be better spent on the subject of the lesson. I am not saying that school uniforms should not be used but I find myself questioning whether they really contribute anything to the school. However, I must say that I like the fact that English teachers always dress smartly. There is something about the English attitude that says 'we are at a place of work now, and therefore we dress properly. We also expect our students to do the same'. In Sweden you may find a teacher who is dressed in jeans and a T-shirt.

Musical Futures

A great approach that I want to bring home and incorporate in my teaching in Swedish schools is the idea of Musical Futures. As I understand it, the aim of Musical Futures is to make music learning as practical as possible. According to the Musical Futures' home page, it is 'a new way of thinking about music-making in schools that brings non-formal teaching and informal learning approaches into the more formal context of schools'[2]. This is done by taking music relevant to the students and using it in the classroom. The big idea with Musical Futures is to make students more interested in music so they want to continue with it at GCSE and A level. What I like about the Musical Futures is that the students seem to become fully engaged in their projects. From what I saw at one of my placement schools in England, all the students were really involved throughout the whole process, from choosing which song a group should play, to helping out with how to play different parts, to performing it, and afterwards evaluating it.

Conclusion

During my time in England I gained a lot of experience which really broadened my view on teaching and I am happy that I was able to learn about a school system which was completely new to me. As I have pointed out, there are similarities and differences between the Swedish and the English systems and I am sure that my insights into both of them will help me develop more in my future role as a teacher. In England we spoke a lot about formal, informal and non-formal learning. It is important to remember that children learn new things at all times, and so do we.

I hope that both England and Sweden can learn from each other. One thing that I would like to see incorporated into the Swedish music teacher education is the involvement of the placement school. I would also like to see the QTS standards used more during the Swedish placement. As mentioned before, I believe that having these standards and making the students provide proof of achieving them, makes the student reflect more upon how to achieve the criteria and should make them into a better teacher.

As I wrote earlier, the lessons in England are planned in more detail. But not only do you need a good structure for your lesson; you also need to let your students know of this structure: how the lesson will start and end, for example. During one lecture at the university in England, I also learnt the importance of letting the students know what they are being assessed on. Assessment should not be a guessing game.

To conclude, I would like to say to anyone who has been thinking about going abroad to study or work: do it. Experience is something that no one can ever take away from you and you will gain much knowledge. Also, you will be very happy that you went. I know I am.

Endnotes

[1] www.oecd.org/dataoecd/54/12/46643496.pdf
[2] www.musicalfutures.org.uk/about

The international student forum: a supportive way to develop the professional profile of future music teachers

Branka Rotar Pance and Gerhard Sammer

> *Loved the whole experience.*
>
> *I think it is very important to meet such a variety of people from different countries — it's very inspirative, brings to us new ideas and thoughts to develop our teaching and improve things.*
>
> *Thoroughly enjoyable, rewarding process, which I now feel is essential for teachers of all subjects to do within Europe and also within the individual countries!!*
>
> (Student feedback, EAS SF 2006b)

Introduction

The European Association for Music in Schools (EAS) considers students in training to be a vital part of the music education profession both as teachers and future researchers. Their current experience in training and their often very recent experience as learners in school make them an important source of feedback on current practices, as well as new thinking and new practices. (Hennessy & Sammer, 2008: 277)

The activities of the EAS, related to European music education, cover a range of forms. One of these is the international EAS student forum (EAS SF), which has been developed over more than ten years and focuses on the student teacher voice. It was established to address:

- the need to develop music education for young people which is challenging, transforming and engaging
- the need to develop the professional knowledge of future teachers in ways that support critical reflection, peer learning and creative thinking

- the importance of cultural, professional and social understanding to facilitate exchange, flexibility and mobility

We have learned that such international meetings can have a strong impact on future music teachers, as evident in the written feedback of the participants over the years. The EAS student forum was developed with a dynamic and open-ended format, and we present its aims, history, concepts, outcomes and future perspectives here.

Aims of the international EAS student forum

The international EAS SF provides students opportunities for sharing knowledge and experience of music education in schools and music teacher training programmes across Europe. The SF is motivated by several aims (Niermann, Malmberg & Sammer, 2008):

- to give students, future music teachers, an opportunity to meet on the international level, share multifaceted perspectives from different countries and institutions and work together on selected professional topics
- to gain new knowledge/competences through thematic lectures, workshops and discussions, led by experts
- to give students an opportunity to share and exchange information, experience and ideas about music in schools, the significance of music education in their own country and about their own music teacher training
- to give students an opportunity to share examples of musical activities and repertoire from their own context and reflect on methods/ways to include those activities in their teaching
- to learn from each other and reflect on the different perspectives on musical learning (in school)
- to stimulate students to develop ideas and be involved in creative work in different group forms
- to support students' professional development
- to develop visions on different aspects regarding music in school within international groups and present the results to a professional community
- to give students an experience on the fascination and challenge of educational and cultural diversity and develop understanding and valuation for foreign positions
- to enable students to present the process and results of the SF and join the EAS network
- to develop a student network for music education in schools all over Europe
- to motivate students to participate on the annual EAS-conference and meet music educators from all over Europe

Between 2006 and 2009 EAS was working on the meNet Project. One of the elements of this project was to develop learning outcomes for music teacher training, to support the development of training across Europe (meNet 2009: 27). The students attending forum events were a valuable source of ideas and feedback in this process; and the final document contributes to the framing and formulation of content for each forum.

History of the international EAS student forum

In 2012 the tenth international EAS SF took place at the annual EAS conference. The first EAS SF was organized in 2001 in Toblach (Italy) over two days by Josef Scheidegger and Franz Niermann (both, now, past presidents of EAS) who conceived the initiative for students in different institutions for music teacher training from Germany, Austria and Slovakia. The students worked together to explore and debate a current issue and their conclusions were presented to the conference and published in German in the conference proceedings (AGMÖ, 2002: 362–363).

The development from this first meeting to the second forum in 2003 was quite a big step. The range was extended to students from 17 universities in six different countries who worked for five days in Salzburg and Vienna. A poster session, workshop and cultural activities were included.

In the third forum, which was held in 2005 in Prague, students from 12 European countries participated in discussions on different aspects regarding the challenges of the Bologna process and the development of the *European University Sphere*. A written report on their conclusions is available on the EAS website and the students argued, as in previous meetings, for more teaching practice in their training (EAS SF, 2005: 3).

For the fourth forum at the University of Music in Würzburg (Germany) the concept and programme were further developed: on the one hand to give impulses through practical music-making workshops and an input session from an EAS board member to frame the topic and stimulate and facilitate discussion; and on the other hand to make sure that the process strengthened the exchange and quality of the students' independent group work. Students were also given opportunities to share their own musical ideas and materials with each other. There was also a greater emphasis on the preparation process of the participants some weeks before the meeting (articles to read in advance, posters etc.) with a focus on the key questions:

- What should be the aims of a 21st-century curriculum for music and how should these aims be achieved?
- In what ways does the curriculum you are trained to teach offer a good foundation for a 21st-century music education for young people?

In a lively presentation to the conference, the students emphasized creativity and the necessity of educating the whole child (EAS SF 2006a).

The forum in 2007 took place in the north of Sweden (Pitea) with a smaller group of participants and worked on the question: what are the future perspectives of music education regarding media and new technology? (EAS SF, 2007) One year later the forum was held in conjunction with the ISME Conference in Bologna, Italy. The students mainly discussed the topic 'Changing music teaching in a time of ongoing globalization' and met in a common session with the members of the ISME Young Professionals Focus Group (EAS SF, 2008).

The seventh forum took place in the 'singing country', Estonia and, as it had become a tradition to link the main theme of the conference to the SF, the forum focused on two different meanings of 'voice': on the one hand the students were invited to take part in a very practical approach with a workshop on vocal improvisation techniques and opportunities to share songs; and on the other hand they discussed the idea of 'student voice' in music education. As expected, in many countries music is still a subject in formal education that is quite dominated by the music teacher — perhaps more so than in other arts subjects. This topic was relatively challenging to students from different countries.

Bolu (Turkey) was the host city for the forum in 2010. The international student group worked intensively on the topic 'Bringing the outside in — the teacher's role in reflecting the musical lives of young people in classroom practice'. One particpant, Jaroslava Lojdova, summarized the most important outcomes of the forum:

> Interaction and mutual co-operation between a teacher and students is a means of meeting their needs and interests. An idea of pupils as experts is also very interesting. [. . .] Then there is space for students to learn together and from each other. (Lojdova, 2010)

The 2011 forum in Gdansk, Poland, was the first time we included two students in the planning group. The forum focused on 'Teacher responsibilities for children's music activity: teaching styles and teachers' roles'. Discussions were related to the practice of the *contemporary* music teacher and the different school contexts and backgrounds in EU countries.

The tenth forum (EAS SF, 2012) was held at the Royal Conservatoire of the Hague. Students shared examples of musical activities in schools, presented their educational systems and worked on the main theme 'Teacher as Musician — the School Perspective'. Students expressed their thinking and visions in different ways: musically, with images and with words, as in these examples:

> *Music teachers should make children feel like artists.* (Samuel)

> *Music teachers should not only be professional and active musicians but also great with pedagogic. Flexible, open-minded, creative, passionate and these are only a few qualities that music teacher should have.* (Subgroup of the EAS SF participants)

Concept and working phases

The EAS SF concept has developed over several years and is designed, organized and led by a team consisting of EAS board members and ordinary members. The SF team also invites different experts (usually from the host country) to lead practical workshops Since 2011 we have extended the SF team to include two student delegates: one selected from the past SF and one from the next host country. This gives students a stronger 'voice' inside the EAS board which co-opts them for one year. Student delegates are engaged in all phases of preparation, execution and evaluation of the SF.

They stimulate further communication between the SF participants after the event and connect the EAS board and the members with future music teachers.

The participants in the EAS SF are nominated through the EAS network of National Coordinators (NCs). There are many advantages of having a strong link to national representatives across Europe. Without them it would be difficult to get in contact with interested and capable students from so many different countries (Niermann, Malmberg & Sammer, 2008: 363). Each NC can nominate one or two students from different teacher training institutions. The host country can nominate up to six students. The participants should be in the final years of their training to become a class music teacher in primary or secondary schools, be interested in European and international perspectives in music education and be able to prepare some materials in advance for the meeting. They should also be able to communicate in English, to work with others and contribute to the debate. The maximum number of participating students is 30.

To achieve the goals and meet the demands of the schedule, participants are led through an intensive working process which starts six weeks before the event. Students are asked to prepare a poster with the main information about music education and teacher training in their country, to bring musical activities to exchange and to read some short texts on the topic before the event.

The SF normally lasts for four days, beginning with structured and moderated activities and a lot of exchange and tasks in different groups. This gradually gives the students more responsibility to decide about the methods, groupings and content on their own. The SF ends with a group presentation at the EAS conference and a final evaluative reflection. The forum's main theme and key questions are always strongly connected to the EAS conference. The schedule also includes an opportunity to meet with the EAS board, as well as social meetings with the participants of the EAS doctoral student forum or the other young professional groups and representatives of other associations connected with music education. There are also organized visits to some tourist attractions and opportunities for the host students to offer some social activities.

The final presentation at the EAS conference is based on the independent and creative group work and lasts about 45 minutes. The presentation acts as a very important impulse for the working process and demands positive engagement from each participant in team work, sharing and accepting ideas and democratic co-operation in the international group. The focus of these presentations is not to present perfect results but to give an insight into the different perspectives, the development of the discussions, the process and some agreed visions. Sometimes the students formulated declarations related to music education in schools, music teacher training programmes, musical practice outside and inside school, music between tradition and globalization and other topics related to educational policy. The developing nature of the SF leads us to new forms of presentation, not just at the EAS conferences but also in connection with other international organizations and networks with 'youth' sections. One student, Agnieszka Lewoc, described her experience:

> I didn't realize that preparing such a short presentation is so time consuming, but I feel it wasn't waste of time. We divided the work between

us and everybody tried to be organized and have some contribution in the presentation. What really surprised me was positive attitude of the people. I was happy that despite of being tired nobody gave up and hardly anyone complained. (Lewoc, 2010)

Evaluation and outcomes

The results from past years confirm that the aims of the forum are well met and that our approach supports students in their development as teachers as reflected in the document *Learning Outcomes in Music Teacher Training* (meNet, 2009). The quality of the SF is first evaluated through analysis of feedback from the participants, comments from National Coordinators, EAS board members and guest experts, and the evaluation of the SF team members. For the last two years we have also used student diaries for monitoring and evaluating the process during the event. The diary method includes guidelines and questions related to expectations, experiences and reflections on the different activities in the programme. Participants write about their feelings and their ideas on how to apply their new experiences and new knowledge in their professional development. They also offer ideas for the further development of the SF and how the group can stay connected after the meeting.

The analysis of all activities and student feedback shows that within the forum it is possible to identify different phases, which are relevant for the individuals and the whole group—all the following examples of reflections are taken from students' diaries in 2012:

At the beginning of the event the students are very enthusiastic and curious and have a positive attitude:

> *It's the first time I go alone to such an event and I'm happy about being accepted and being part of this harmonic and creative group of international students . . .* (Leonie)

> *I really enjoyed the warm-up activities and felt they were a great way to get to know everybody.* (Sophie)

> *The atmosphere was great, friendly and family-like. Our group work was top-class. What I expected I met it.* (Mariusz)

> *I already learned a lot of things and I'm looking forward to learn some more. It's hard to think and speak in English but I'll get to use it. I hope there will be even more singing and warm-up games and I'm very excited about tomorrow and some new activities.* (Andreja)

Later on, the participants are still strongly engaged and interested in different activities related to the sharing and learning, while exchanging musical activities and learning from each other:

> *I particularly enjoyed sharing and learning the new songs and activities. It was great to perform and then enjoy everyone else performances.* (Katherine)

> *I enjoyed during singing songs from other countries. I also really enjoyed at workshops—I hope I wrote down everything because I don't want to forget anything—I want to use all ideas!* (Maša)
>
> *I've learned that we can create music nearly from nothing. That simple tasks or patterns can create something great. I've got to know many interesting exercises.* (Mariusz)
>
> *The school systems are so different. There was not enough time to discuss details.* (Natascha)

To organize and communicate the independent group-work within a limited time in such a big international group is of course a big challenge for the students. When they start to collate the ideas from group work into a single presentation for the conference some students change their mood. They report excited, insecure feelings, tiredness, issues about the subgroup structure and compatibility with the other group members, the working balance in the group in respect of individuals' capacities for productive team-work or problems with some inner 'leaders', language problems in communication, etc:

> *I feel a little bored and kind of stressed because we didn't understand each other very well. At the end we worked out quite well, but beginnings wasn't easy. I had higher expectation, so I felt silly with my offers.* (Liama)
>
> *Today was really tiring, we argued a bit today in our group, main problem were structure and decisions . . .* (Eveline)
>
> *General atmosphere: very good. Subgroups: it is starting to be clear that there are some dominant personalities, that we have some difficulties accepting other ideas, what might lead to some little frustrations. But I think that's natural.* (Hans)

In the end, when the students have presented the results of their work on the stage to the main conference, they always express their satisfaction with this experience at the final plenary meeting.

> *I feel happy. After the stressy and 'unhappy' day yesterday we present a good work.* (Leonie)
>
> *I'm relieved! I think it went much better than I expected. I was scared that maybe it would be too 'childish' for the audience, but in such a short time it was really the best we could do. I think that we showed them very well what we were doing and our results. I'm glad that we got much positive feedback.* (Irina)

From the written reflections of the participants we are also able to analyse personal expectations, experiences and reflections on the working tasks and forms, and difficulties in the working process.

Expectations

> *I expect that I'll get some new ideas for my own classes. I also hope that we will have fun and that I'll learn more about school systems in other countries.* (Andreja)

> *I'd like to explore different ideas and methods in music pedagogy.* (Kristine)

> *Inspiration and connections are my main interest.* (Eveline)

> *To get a global image of the music education in Europe. Second, to get some more social contacts in the music education in Europe and learn new songs of different countries.* (Maarten)

Experiences and reflections

> *I learned many things, especially from the workshop. How to work with the group of people — how to entertain and to do music at the same time. I enjoyed the process of creation, to make something from one idea. It was surprising that how people from so different countries can understand everyone in musical language.* (Kristine)

> *I like that the subgroups are mixed up so we can talk and work with almost everyone.* (Sarah)

> *The group-work isn't easy for me (in Czech Republic group work isn't very common in schools) but I consider it very valuable.* (Petr)

> *I like that you learn a lot from this work with people that you don't know very well and in the end we had a total performance. And it's not about the final presentation but about the process and this you learn most from.* (Meike)

> *A group-process is possible even if the people in the group have many different ideas!* (Judith)

Difficulties in the working process

> *Sometimes it's difficult when we learn to teach some song in a different language.* (Radka)

> *It was always such a short time we had to work in the groups.* (Judith)

> *The day is so long, it's difficult to stay concentrated all day.* (Leonie)

> *Making a performance with a group in a short time. Everyone had a lot of ideas and songs.* (Maarten)

> *It was very difficult to develop the ideas because everyone had another vision of the final performance. So we spend a lot of time with discussing.*

> *But when the general idea was more clear it was very interesting to see how all the ideas also of the other groups become one final big performance and idea.* (Julia)

Some students wrote reports for their national music journals or university publications. We can review the outcomes through texts such as Imre's:

> During the week I realized that because of the forum, I mostly learned to reflect on the music education in my own country [. . .] The cultural differences became not only visible in the musical differences, but also in the way the students tried to find a consensus or even try to focus on the difference in the discussions. (Ploeg, 2011)

The international SF opens several channels for professional communication based on respect for different traditions, cultural and educational contexts in various regions and countries. Long discussions between the participants during the event are often connected with the clarification of terminology. Explaining in English is for some students still a big problem and an obstacle to communication. It is also apparent that professional terminology differs in some countries and this is especially connected to their educational tradition, context and educational philosophy. The necessity to communicate mainly in a foreign language is, of course, also a disadvantage for the quality of the conversation.

Some participants suggested reducing the number of participating countries, which would give us the opportunity to go deeper into discussion about national educational systems and music teacher training programmes in the participating countries. But this means a loss of diversity of perspectives and the opportunity to share professional knowledge and experiences in a broad international dimension.

Working with culturally and linguistically mixed groups differs every time. It is important that tutors are strict in time-keeping and, from the beginning, help to strengthen the awareness of everyone's responsibility for balanced communication, to avoid dominance by some eloquent students and to ensure the involvement of every student within plenary discussions and subgroup work. The SF is a good opportunity to monitor students' readiness for team working, their flexibility, working styles, different approaches and values. This attitude is also connected to the diversity of the participants' institutions, as music teacher training programmes are implemented at universities, music conservatories, music academies, high schools of music, faculties of arts, faculties of education, colleges of music teacher education and within specialist music teacher training courses. Such institutions differ in their organization and the structure of their curricula for music teacher training. Diversity is seen in the balance between artistic subjects, music theory/music science subjects and pedagogy subjects in their music teacher training programmes (Gall et al., 2011; Rotar Pance, 2012a). Some institutions are more focused on popular music, others on classical music, jazz or traditional music. There are evident differences between systems of teaching practice and the position of research work in teacher training programmes. Diverse backgrounds and educational values are presented and connected in the forum. This influences all working phases and especially that of preparing the presentation for the conference stage. Students' reflections afterwards and feedback from the audience after the performance should also be seen through this perspective. 'These reflections help us not only to learn about each other but also suggest the ways in which we can learn from each other' (Gall et al., 2011: 342). For future music teachers we are trying to find new approaches to music education.

Future vision of the student network

The international EAS student forum highlights and stimulates multicultural forms of learning and enables an interaction between music education theory and practice, focused on specific topics. It supports individual personal growth and the professional development of the participants through different working forms and specific tasks An interesting option for its future development is to organize regional SFs, prepared by EAS NCs which could be linked to the international EAS SF.

New social media (e.g. Facebook) give us the opportunity to build the SF network, so that former participants can keep connected through particular SF groups which could also be open for new interested students. This is a possible way of addressing the need, expressed by some of the SF participants:

> It would be very good for the students of each forum to be able to come twice to a forum like that [. . .] One year is not enough, it is just an idea. But if they come twice then they could have a picture of what is happening, and thus learn more, and have the opportunity to bring new ideas in the next year. (Amaryllis, EAS SF, 2003)

The main strategy of the EAS SF is that students participate once at the event because we would like to give this experience to many students from different institutions and countries. We would also like the students to stay connected after finishing their study and starting work as music teachers. Therefore the network would develop automatically into a European music teacher network. A vision of the EAS SF is to build a lively platform for music teachers and students, exchanging experiences, sharing materials, discussing professional topics and issues, finding project partners and supporting the mobility of each individual.

References:

AGMÖ (Arbeitsgemeinschaft der Musikerzieher Österreichs); Institut für Musikerziehung in deutscher und ladinischer Sprache (2002) *Warum nicht Musik ?! [Why not Music?!]* Bozen/Wien: AGMÖ Publications series Vol. 24: 353–364.

EAS SF (2003) Evaluation of the EAS SF 2003 in Salzburg/Vienna. Unpublished documents.

EAS SF (2005) [online]. Available at www.eas-music.org/activities/student-forum-sf/archive/2005-prague-cz/ (accessed 07/08/12).

EAS SF (2006a) Unprinted manuscript of the students presentation in Würzburg.

EAS SF (2006b) Evaluations of the EAS SF 2006 in Würzburg. Unpublished documents.

EAS SF (2007) [online]. Available at www.eas-music.org/activities/student-forum-sf/archive/2007-pitea-se/ (accessed 15/08/12).

EAS SF (2008) [online]. Students statements on the use of new media in the field of music teaching reflecting the national perspective. Available at www.eas-music.org/activities/student-forum-sf/2008-bologna-it/ (accessed 15/08/12).

EAS SF (2012) [online]. Available at www.eas-music.org/activities/student-forum-sf/2012-the-hague-nl/ (accessed 10 July 2012).

Gall, M. et al. (2011) Learning from each other: music teacher training in Europe with a special focus on England, Slovenia, Sweden and Germany. In A. Liimets & M. Mäesalu (eds.) *Music inside and outside the school* (Baltische Studien zur Erziehungs- und Sozialwissenschaft, Bd. 21). Frankfurt am Main, Peter Lang, 325–344.

Hennessy, S. & Sammer, G. (2008) EAS Student forum. In: Abstracts, 28th ISME World Conference. Music at all ages. (20–25 July 2008. Bologna, Italy), 277, 278.

Lewoc, A. (2010) 9th International EAS Student Forum Gdansk, Poland 2011. [Online]. Available at www.eas-music.org/activities/student-forum-sf/2011-gdansk-pl/report/ (accessed 08/08/12).

Lojdova, J. (2010) EAS Student Forum and Conference in Bolu, Turkey 2010 [online]. Available at www.eas-music.org/activities/student-forum-sf/2010-bolu-turkey/ (accessed 15/08/12).

meNet [Music Education Network] (2009) *Learning Outcomes in Music Teacher Training.* Wien: Institut für Musikpädagogik. Available at www.menet.info (accessed 15/08/12).

Niermann, F., Malmberg, I. & Sammer, G. (2008) Netzwerk-Arbeit für musikalische Bildung in Europa. Aktuelle Themenschwerpunkte der EAS. In: H. Bäßler & O. Nimczik (eds.) *Stimme(n). Kongressbericht der 26. Bundesschulmusikwoche Würzburg 2006.* Mainz: Schott-Verlag 361–387.

Ploeg, I. (2011) *EAS Student Forum 2011 Gdansk.* [online]. Available at http://kunstzone.nl/magazines/kunstzone-2011/juli-augustus/eas-student-forum-2011-gdansk-1 (accessed 20/07/12).

Rotar Pance, B. (2012, in press) Training and professional profile of music teachers. In: O. Denac (ed.) *New Perspectives in Music Education in Slovenia.* Hauppage, NY: Nova Science Publishers.

Section 2

Perspectives on teaching and learning

It's better in the Bahamas

Daniel Knight

All around the world, you've got to spread the word
Tell them what you heard
You know it's gonna be OK
                        Noel Gallagher (released 1998)

In 1985 The Commonwealth Heads of Government conference was hosted by the Bahamas. Queen Elizabeth II opened the conference and afterwards undertook a number of public engagements. My school's choir was invited to sing at one of these. It was to be held outside (in the blazing sun) at the opening of a new housing social suburb, *Elizabeth Estates,* intended to help clear some of Nassau's slums. I remember thinking after the performance that the chance of this happening in a typical UK school was extremely remote. So teaching abroad can have unexpected benefits. This chapter is not intended as a guide to teaching music abroad; I simply offer a few experiences of my own that may prove to be enlightening to someone about to embark on this kind of adventure and to raise some of the issues involved. Working abroad can be exciting. Moreover, the perception of teaching music in an exotic location can be very tempting. It can however be fraught with danger. Stepping into the unknown can feel like falling into the abyss.

Into the Sudan

My story begins with the back pages of the *TES* (*Times Educational Supplement*) where I saw my first overseas job as a volunteer English teacher in a High School in Kassala, Sudan. I knew that Sudan was ranked near the bottom of the list of the poorest countries and that 'voluntary' was code for subsistence-level pay and even scarcer teaching resources. It was going to be a challenge but it was better than being unemployed.

At a weekend in the glamorous surroundings of Farnham Castle in Surrey, a group of about 30 graduates, about to leave for Khartoum, were treated to dining-room meals and a crash course in teaching English as a Foreign Language (EFL). It was an immense contrast to the conditions we found ourselves in a few weeks later. With some pocket money and another short EFL course at the British Council in Khartoum, the year began for a group of graduates with no teaching qualifications being posted to the four corners of the country.

The school I was assigned to had an average class size of 80. The text books included 'The Nile Course for the Sudan' (Longman) and simplified works of literature. I was asked to teach them *The Mill on the Floss*. I don't think they could have chosen anything more culturally remote. I have to admit that the quality of the teaching didn't rise much above sea-level but the enthusiasm of the students made up for the lack of resources and the large classes.

By sharing accommodation with seven other teachers who were assigned to different schools in the town, we saved money and lived a fairly comfortable existence. The only contact with the outside world was a shortwave radio and a Sony Walkman. However, it gave me time to reflect, take a break from music and the four hours of piano practice a day, read some books and consider teaching as a realistic career.

Most people (including me) managed to last out one academic year but couldn't wait to return home. I returned to the UK, completed a PGCE and immediately began work as a class teacher in a primary school in London. This lasted a year before I started looking at the overseas pages in the *TES* again.

Nassau

> *If you don't know where you are going, any road will take you there.*
> Lewis Carroll: Alice in Wonderland (1885)

When I boarded the plane to Miami in 1984 and headed to the Bahamas, little did I realize I was going to make this place my home for the next eleven years. 'It's better in the Bahamas' was the slogan the Ministry of Tourism used to promote the country around the world and at first glance there is some truth in the statement. The beaches were first class; the sea was a translucent turquoise; the whole place was ringed with palm trees; rum was cheap and partying was a way of life. The climate was perfect all year round. The soca, calypso and reggae were as intoxicating as the rum and it was truly a fun place. However, in reality the Bahamas is a third-world country. The economy is heavily dependent on tourism and, with a small population of just about 300,000 people, the tax base is so small that the government coffers have to rely entirely on indirect purchase taxes. This makes the cost of living very high.

Moving countries, jobs and house all at once can be extremely stressful for people, as they step out of their comfort zone and into the unknown. This is one of the reasons that international schools generally offer some sort of orientation or induction programme. the Bahamas had a 'do-it-yourself' approach. There was no real induction programme and the month's salary cheque they gave us in order to rent a place to live had to be paid back over the coming year.

The school I was assigned to was a state primary school with 1,200 students. Classes were a reasonable 30 students per class but in order for all of them to have a music lesson once a week the classes had to be paired. I walked in on my first day feeling quite nervous: I don't know quite what I expected, but when the students came together for the first assembly and I saw 1,200 little bright faces staring back at me, I felt a little discombobulated. I was faced with large classes, almost no resources, absolutely no budget and an expectation to put on public performances.

Music teachers working abroad may find themselves in culturally precarious territory, knowing little about the local culture but still expected to teach their subject in a way that is relevant to the community. I needed to find out more about the traditions of the school and discovered quite quickly the existence of a deeply entrenched evangelical Christian ethos. It became clear that a large part of my time would be spent teaching Christian hymns and songs. Morning worship (many songs and choruses) and the daily singing of the national anthem were central to the music education. At that time, the state education system had no written curriculum, so as long as I managed to play up to twelve songs or hymns by ear in an assembly and direct large gospel choirs, I was left to teach what I liked.

I found myself in a bit of a musical quandary: I had come from a musical tradition where everything is written down but now found myself working with people who had much more of an oral musical culture. The musical traditions of the Bahamians reflect their history — the sacred music of the Baptist tradition; the secular music of calypso, soca and reggae. The teaching staff were highly gifted musically and would often sing solos in front of the school while their class assemblies resembled mass gospel choirs and sounded amazing. I had to learn how to play by ear and to remember arrangements of gospel songs we had worked out together. It was in many ways a collegial learning environment. They guided me through their music so I could eventually turn up to rehearsals knowing that there would be no written scores but that we would work through each piece until we had the arrangement they wanted. The children's songs were more like Sunday school choruses and easily remembered and performed.

The most prominent music festival in the islands is Junkanoo, which takes place on Christmas night and Boxing Day morning and consists mainly of elaborate homemade costumes combined with a carnival around central Nassau to the beat of homemade Goombay (goatskin) drums. Similar celebrations once existed across the Caribbean and in North Carolina, but are now virtually extinct except in the Bahamas and Belize. Junkanoo was embraced by the whole school community and, while not directly part of my teaching, the drumming skills learned outside school by some students were something I could draw on during performances of local songs with the school choirs.

A steel band and a string ensemble

The scarcity of resources and large classes meant that it was impossible to engage in practical instrumental lessons. The Ministry of Education decided (always a top-down approach) that they should have a more focused music curriculum and bought parts of the new Silver Burdett Music Scheme but failed to buy sufficient pupil books or CDs so it was again extremely difficult to implement. However, it did provide at least some guidance, in terms of scope and sequence, that was previously lacking.

After many years of working there and having no instruments to play, I discovered a somewhat dilapidated steel band in the attic of the school. At around the same time I found out about ten violins that the Ministry of Education had purchased but which nobody wanted. Although I had never had a lesson in my life, I took on both sets of instruments. I got hold of a Suzuki School for the Violin Book One and started to teach myself. I then set up a small free Saturday morning music school. Inevitably this grew to 15 then 20 violins as I solicited donations from the richer sectors of the community. The violins made their debut at an inter-school Ministry of Education Carol Service in Nassau Cathedral and were an instant hit. The proximity of the Bahamas to the USA (less than 200 miles from Nassau to Miami) creates opportunities for educational exchange programmes and one day a high school orchestra from Charlotte, North Carolina, asked if they could perform at a local school in Nassau. We soon formed a relationship with them that led to our young fiddle players performing at a Blue Grass Fiddle Festival at Union Grove in North Carolina.

I spent eleven wonderful years in the Bahamas. It is a hard place to leave but my time had come to move on. After island life, I needed to live in a city with lots of people and by sheer luck landed a job in Bangkok at a recently (1995) opened International School.

Thailand

> *One night in Bangkok makes a hard man humble*
> *Not much between despair and ecstasy*
> *One night in Bangkok and the tough guys tumble*
> *Can't be too careful with your company*
> *I can feel the devil walking next to me*
> Tim Rice: Chess (1984)

After the tranquillity of the Bahamas, arriving in a teeming oriental city like Bangkok was exhilarating and exciting. I was to work in an 'International School': at last — a place with small class sizes and proper teaching resources. The year was 1995 and it was my first encounter with the internet. This single innovation would revolutionize music education and how we teach music forever. The slow dial-up connection to the internet at that time was as good as it got and we were years away from programmes like Sibelius and YouTube, but as I stood in my new music room in Bangkok I was delighted.

Traditionally, international schools provided an education for children whose parents were stationed abroad for employment purposes. These would generally be British children who would be returning to the UK to live and would attend the local school without missing a beat. That reality had now changed: the Thai government, in response to a rising middle class demand for private education, had amended the law so that Thai children could opt out of the state system and attend local private schools. In an increasingly globalized world, more wealthy Thai parents wanted their children educated in English.

Education in Thailand in 1995 included provision for the arts as a foundation subject in schools, but its implementation was somewhat uneven. However, international schools generally employed specialist music teachers in the primary sector and the emphasis and value placed on music was central to their existence. While public exams and university placements were also important, music was often the prism through which parents would see the success of a school.

So the student body at this school (and dozens of international schools across Thailand) consisted mainly of Thai children who were Buddhist, while the curriculum was based largely on the national curriculum of England with some adaptation to local conditions.

Some areas of the curriculum were of dubious relevance (a study of a farm in Surrey) but the main challenge wasn't the content of the curriculum but the language: English was a second language to nearly all the students. The language at home was Thai; the language of the playground was Thai; the language of the country was Thai, so the only place English was encountered was in the classroom. I was able to draw on the knowledge that one of the main activities in music — singing — aids language development in many ways: songs are a form of poetry and singing words can disguise a spoken accent; this enhances verbal language while at the same time advancing student's musical language. There are challenges however in the choice of songs to use in school. I found a balance between international folk songs and modern popular songs often worked well with older students, while songs which modelled singing with recorded examples (as found in published music schemes) were helpful in providing access for students less proficient in English.

Teaching songs was a way into English but at least instrumental music was a universal language. A large number of students had music lessons outside school, usually geared towards the ABRSM and Trinity graded exams, and could play the piano: this made composition classes easier. Building up a tradition of anything in an entirely new school is both exciting and extremely challenging. Exciting because anything you do is new and challenging because you are responsible for the public face of the school and have to ensure that standards are high.

At first musical performances were limited to class assemblies, but as the school moved into the secondary phase there were opportunities to make links between music and drama and develop more sophisticated performances. As the school developed it introduced the International General Certificate of Secondary Education (IGCSE). I was to teach the first year 10–11 cohort. I decided that the GCSE (OCR) was a more appropriate curriculum for my students than the IGCSE (Cambridge) which has a more traditional approach with set works from the classical tradition. The OCR had a more practical approach enabling students to make their own choice of performances, including rock, Thai or classical, and this enabled them to be more successful. One of the challenges of working in a growing international school is the ability to teach across the age range. I would teach a class of year 1 students for a period and then find myself in front of a year 11 class. It was assumed that if you have the subject knowledge you can teach any age group.

My new school had been intended to grow into an 'all-through' school (reception–sixth form) over a period of six years. There was a promise of a new purpose-built campus and plans for the building were advanced when the Asian financial crisis hit in 1997 and the Thai currency collapsed. The new campus was put on hold and eventually cancelled. The Head left and the new management were unable to maintain the exponential growth of the school. An opportunity to work at Seoul Foreign School meant that I would leave Thailand after five wonderful years. I had used the time to learn to speak Thai and to bring a new music department into being having completed its first GCSE course.

The land of morning calm

South Korea is known as the 'land of the morning calm' although the city of Seoul is more like the land of morning chaos! In the northern part of the city, high on a hill in Yonhi Dong, is Seoul Foreign School. It is a conglomeration of four schools under one umbrella — three American and one British. Although Seoul Foreign School was founded in 1912, the British School was added as recently as 1982. The student body was largely expatriate families from the UK or the EU, in Seoul for a limited time. One of the consequences of this was the students rarely stayed at the school for more than three years (the length of a typical posting).

The need to cater for expatriate students meant that the British School offered an education based on the national curriculum of England. The use of the national curriculum and its associated assessment tools such as SATs at 7, 11 and 14 enabled parents to get an idea of their child's progress and made it easier for them to transfer out of Korea and return home with relatively little disruption.

When I arrived at the British School there was no real musical tradition or expectation other than to teach the classes and round up a choir to sing Christmas carols at various venues around Seoul, including the UK Ambassador's residence. The music department had been somewhat neglected with the allocation of just a part-time teacher before me, so I had the task of building it virtually from scratch. This school, too, was growing into a secondary school and I would eventually be teaching right across the age range. This time, though, I had unprecedented facilities and was able to be part of a much larger music faculty. I was finally going to work in a school where funding was practically unlimited.

Being part of a larger, mainly American campus, I was able to observe the American music curriculum at close quarters for the first time and found it extremely enlightening. Performance is central to their curriculum and they do it very well. Choirs, bands and orchestras are on the timetable and not pushed to the periphery of the extra-curricular programme as they could be in the British system. Purpose-built choir and orchestra classrooms and modern concert halls are part of the music education landscape where performances can be presented to parents in a professional environment. Inspired by this example, I was able to start a British School orchestra and introduce a tradition of each key stage presenting a musical for the parents once a year.

However, there was a clear lack of creative music-making in the American curriculum, with no room for composition or learning about music technology. The narrowness of this curriculum can lead to problems with post-16 students studying for IB music where there is a requirement for both individual composition and passing a listening paper. As an IB examiner for the performance exam at Seoul Foreign School I came across anecdotal evidence to suggest that students felt unprepared for these aspects of the examination whilst receiving close to full marks for performance.

One of the defining issues in music education is the isolation of the teachers in their departments but also within the wider profession. The ubiquity of British Schools across Asia led to the development of FOBISSEA (the Federation of British Schools in South East Asia), which formalized ties and created sporting and cultural links. FOBISSEA initiated an annual music festival and the first attended by my students was held in Kuala Lumpur. While I was in South Korea I hosted this event in our new ten million dollar performing arts centre. It was a great opportunity to meet colleagues across the region and to be part of a professional development network that was supportive for all.

The programme of the music festival consisted mainly of large choir and orchestra pieces as well as chamber groups, and always contained an afternoon of indigenous music of the host country. In Jakarta the students played large gamelan instruments with local musicians' guidance; in Korea they incorporated the traditional *salmanori* drumming into a *nanta* pots and pans performance. The term *nanta* refers to reckless punching, as in a boxing match, so you can expect to see lots of action in a *nanta* performance. The performers on stage portray cooks in a kitchen preparing for a wedding banquet and make use of pots, pans, knives, chopping boards, dishes and all sorts of everyday items as their percussion instruments. Traditional Korean drum beats are incorporated into the music.

In terms of professional development the school was more than generous in offering teachers an individual professional development account and I decided at this time that I wanted to pursue further study. I enrolled in the Education Doctorate programme at the University of Sheffield and spent four years completing it, including a year's sabbatical. It was an exciting and challenging thing to do, but a year away from teaching is a good time to reflect and come back renewed and refreshed. One of the drawbacks of taking the sabbatical was the commitment to remaining at the school for a further two years. It was at this point I decided I wanted another change. I liked Asia but wanted something different. I wanted to live and work in Hong Kong. I left the British School in Seoul with a strong music department with a number of enduring traditions that have enabled it to grow. These included a flourishing orchestra and choir as well as the introduction of annual productions of musicals for all key stages.

Hong Kong

As I sit here writing this, I can see from my 42nd-floor Hong Kong apartment an amazing view; I can also see a view of the past: of all the schools and countries that I have worked in and how, while the job is essentially the same on the surface, it is also defined by the local culture, traditions and ethos of each place. The school I am now working in is filled with highly motivated musically literate children. It is a primary school which is part of the English Schools Foundation (ESF). It doesn't have the facilities I had in Seoul, but the students are probably the most rewarding I have ever worked with. The ESF has a long tradition of education provision in Hong Kong dating back to colonial times where there was a great need for schools delivering a curriculum in English. This has continued under the new system of Chinese rule as Hong Kong is classed as a 'Special Administrative Region'. In reality it means the British have left but nothing else is going to change as long as the city-state continues to remain a major financial hub in Asia.

In an effort to internationalize the schools and shed the ties that made the schools 'British Schools', ESF has moved from the English National Curriculum to the International Baccalaureate (IB) diploma and the Primary Years Programme (PYP) but kept the GCSE since the IBO (International Baccalaureate Organization) does not provide for an examination at 16. The PYP has a lot more in common with the Plowden model of inquiry education than the national curriculum followed in England. In terms of music, the PYP has had a positive effect in that it has moved the performing arts away from the periphery of the curriculum and integrated it to link directly with the work being done in the mainstream classroom. Although we accept that we need to teach 'stand-alone' units that are specific to the subject there is a requirement to take a trans-disciplinary approach where possible. Being part of the ESF is also an opportunity to be part of a community of music educators across Hong Kong and provides students with the kinds of musical experiences offered at county music schools with larger interschool choirs and orchestras. The IBO in turn offers professional development at schools across the Asia Pacific region with staff travelling to a range of countries for workshops and courses. Music teachers often feel isolated in their schools and being able to share ideas, resources and expertise with colleagues is both reassuring and helpful

Beyond educational tourism

Teachers can gain international experience in different ways. One way is to provide opportunities to study abroad (tourist approach); a second model is to work in an international school for expatriate students with a curriculum that is mostly modelled on the UK or North American system, and a third is to work in a local school in another country and immerse yourself not only in the country but also within the schools and the community. As music educators, we have to be constantly vigilant that we can continue 'teaching music musically', where we are concerned with the nature of music itself, its value and metaphorical significance, while being aware of the social context of musical understanding. In other words we need to be aware of where we are at all times in order to make what we teach relevant. We need to develop sensitivity to a culture that is different from our own and shy away from cultural imperialism. Assimilating a new culture as well as in some way imparting it can lead to a deeper rapport with your students. However rewarding the encounter, it can also be extremely challenging and the ability to adapt quickly is essential. The idea that 'this is not the way we do things where I come from' will be unhelpful.

Since the Second World War, the growth in the number of international schools has been exponential. There are now thousands of these schools all over the world. Of course, they are not all the same: some schools are appalling and are driven by profit and where education is at best seen as marginal. Others are amazing—they value staff and offer a truly worthwhile experience; one of the great benefits of this is that while good music teachers are increasingly hard to find it is now possible to live almost anywhere you want to. Like the traveller in the Robert Frost poem *The Road Not Taken* I have had and continue to have a wonderful and enriching experience:

I shall be telling this with a sigh
Somewhere ages and ages hence:
Two roads diverged in a wood, and I—
I took the one less traveled by,
And that has made all the difference.
                              Robert Frost (1874–1963)

Teaching music in different cultural contexts: Japan and England

Tomoko Ogusu

Hearing that I had become a qualified music teacher in England was the happiest moment of my life. It had taken more than ten years for this dream to come true. My journey to explore music education in foreign countries began in 1999 with a two-week study visit to Charles County, Maryland, USA, as part of my music degree course in Japan. I had some experience of music education in Japan as a student and after my graduation I was qualified as a music teacher in Japan. However, reflecting on the music education I saw in the USA prompted me to find out more about music education outside of Japan and what teachers in other countries considered to be the most appropriate approaches to teaching music. Six years later this led to the completion of my Masters thesis at Tokyo Gakugei University: 'A study of Music Standards in Maryland, USA with a focus on Primary Music Education in Charles County.' I visited Charles County again in order to observe music lessons at primary and secondary levels and to interview music teachers. I examined the relationship between the standards at national level (Mahlmann, et al., 1994) state level (Benzil, et al., 1997) and county level (Cooper, et al., 2000). I also compared them to the equivalent requirements in Japan (Monbusyo, The Ministry of Education, 1999a,b). While writing my thesis, I became interested in the question of how music teachers outside of Japan feel about music education in their own countries. I decided I would like to explore this further by becoming a qualified music teacher in an English-speaking country. I spent some time in the Japanese education system, initially at a state school and later at a private English immersion school, where the Japanese-English immersion programmes are offered and 70% of the school curricular activities are taught in English. This experience of multiple teaching methods and class management techniques further motivated me to contribute to the education of children in English. Finally, in 2010, I stepped into school education in the UK starting my PGCE Secondary Music course at Reading University.

I am going to describe some differences between music education in England and Japan as a first step towards understanding and exploring good practice in both countries.

Music curriculum

My biggest concern on starting to teach GCSE music in my second school placement was having to teach music analysis. When I was a music teacher in Japan, what I needed to teach was mainly singing songs and playing instruments, not analysis or composition. The content of the AS/A2-level curriculum in England would be mostly taught at university-level in Japan. I did not study harmony and music analysis, which appear in KS5 in England, until I entered the music degree course of the Department of Education at Bunkyo University in Japan. In England, I have taught composition as well as teaching students to sing songs or play instruments based on written music. At KS3 I have taught a lot of composition and I have taught music analysis at KS4 and KS5. I am now confident to teach music in a style which is a combination of Japanese skill-based music education and English composition-based music education, though in order to do so I needed to understand the conceptual differences between the music curriculums in the two countries.

National Curriculum, England (Primary school, ages 5–11)	Course of Study, Japan (Primary school, ages 6–12)
Teaching should ensure that 'listening, and applying knowledge and understanding', are developed through the interrelated skills of 'performing', 'composing' and 'appraising'.	To encourage pupils to cultivate their sentiments, fundamental abilities for musical activities, a love for music as well as a sensitivity toward it, through music-making and appraising.
England (KS3 Secondary school, ages 11–14)	**Japan (Junior high school, ages 12–15)**
There are a number of key concepts that underpin the study of music. Pupils need to understand these concepts in order to deepen and broaden their knowledge, skills and understanding. 1 Integration of practice 2 Cultural understanding 3 Critical understanding 4 Creativity 5 Communication	To encourage pupils to cultivate their sentiments, a love for music as well as enrich their sensitivity to music, develop fundamental abilities for musical activities and deepen understanding of music culture, through a wide variety of music-making and appraising activities.

Table 1: Overall objectives for music: National Curriculum in England (DfEE, 1999, QCA, 2007) and Course of Study in Japan (MEXT, 2008a,b)

I think that the music curriculum in England aims to enable pupils to understand music in more depth. From my experience as a music teacher in Japan, I think the 'fundamental abilities for musical activities' called for in the Course of Study tend to be developed mostly through performing (singing and playing instruments) and only a little by composing and appraising. With regard to appraising, Japanese music education focuses more on the emotional appreciation of music, such as what you feel when you listen to music, than on analysis using the elements of music. Music education in England focuses in more depth on the elements of music, particularly when it comes to music analysis at GCSE and A level.

England	Japan
Primary school, ages 5–11 1 Controlling sounds through singing and playing — performing skills 2 Creating and developing musical ideas — composing skills 3 Responding and reviewing — appraising skills 4 Listening, and applying knowledge and understanding **Secondary school KS3, ages 11–14** 1 Performing, composing and listening 2 Reviewing and evaluating	**Primary school, ages 6–12;** **Junior high school, ages 12–15** A. Music making 1 Singing* 2 Playing Instruments 3 Creative Music Making B. Appreciation *to include a selection from the Common Materials, prescribed lists of Japanese songs

Table 2: Curriculum content: National Curriculum in England (DfEE, 1999; OCA, 2007) and Course of Study in Japan (MEXT, 2008a,b)

I think that music education in England targets the understanding of real music through a greater emphasis on 'applying knowledge and understanding' at the primary level and 'reviewing and evaluating' at the secondary level. My impression is that it is more challenging to learn music in England than in Japan as pupils are expected to evaluate music analytically and to integrate their performing, composing, and appraising skills. However, I believe that evaluating music using acquired integrated music skills is the only way to achieve real depth of musical understanding. Music teachers in England also need more advanced musical knowledge and skills than those in Japan, in terms of teaching music analytically. If Japanese education were to introduce more music analysis into their curriculum, music teachers in Japan would need further training in how to teach music analysis, especially to pupils at secondary level. When teaching Japanese traditional instruments was introduced into the Course of Study ten years ago, many seminars were provided to prepare music teachers and trainee teachers to teach Japanese traditional instruments which they had never played.

In my experience, teaching music at secondary school (KS3–5, ages 11–18) in England is more daunting than in Japan. This is because Japanese music teachers do not need to teach a wide age range, as they are based in either a junior high school (ages 12–15) or a high school (ages 15–18). Two different teaching licenses are issued in Japan, one for junior high school and another for high school, not simply one teaching qualification for all levels of secondary school as in England.

Differentiation

In England, differentiation is a key issue in planning and teaching lessons. Although my PGCE music tutor explained to us how to incorporate differentiation into our lesson objectives and expected outcomes, I needed a while to understand the concept and use it in my own music teaching. I had never seen such a word when I was a teacher in Japan. Education in Japan is based on a concept of 'equality' whereby all the pupils can achieve the same objectives in each lesson. The outcomes and objectives in lesson plans in Japan are described without differentiation.

Education in England makes much of supporting individual learning. In addition to differentiated objectives and outcomes, lesson plans in England are expected to contain provision for SEN pupils and able (G&T) pupils. These are completely missing from Japanese lesson plans as schools in Japan tend not to identify SEN pupils and G&T pupils in this way, and do not share the information so widely. For instance, when a SEN pupil was in my primary class in Japan, I had a meeting with his parents and shared the provision only with teachers who were involved in his lessons. I was really surprised in England to have access to full details of SEN pupils and able pupils, and to find that SEN pupils often learn particular subjects such as maths and English away from their main classroom. This would not happen in Japanese schools. Even if a SEN pupil in mainstream is weak in maths, teachers tend to keep him/her in the main classroom with a teaching assistant, though a pupil whose mother tongue is not Japanese and who needs to have extra support would receive a special Japanese lesson for a whole period instead of joining the normal Japanese lesson.

I find it really useful to look at information about SEN pupils and G&T pupils before starting to teach, as I can set up the suitable differentiated tasks to support their individual learning in my lesson planning. For instance, during my PGCE, I often made two different worksheets (one for SEN pupils, the other for the rest of pupils) in my music lessons so that SEN pupils could achieve the lesson objectives in their own way within the limited lesson time. In addition, I planned extension tasks for G&T pupils so that they could further their music ability in the same lesson.

In Japan, planning such obviously differentiated tasks for music lessons would not be possible. A good lesson in Japan means that every pupil should strive to achieve the same objectives and the same outcomes. It is seen as a virtue in Japanese society that everyone works or studies equally together towards the same aims. In music lessons in Japan, pupils often practise singing songs and playing instruments together until they can feel 'unity' through the music as an ensemble. Music teachers tend to spend a couple of lessons dealing with only one piece of music in order to raise the level of the performance at the end. Each school holds music concerts in which all the pupils must take part. When I was a junior high school student, I used to take part in these concerts. We spent a lot of time in music lessons rehearsing a song as a choir, as it was a music competition judged by our teachers and our student representatives. One of the purposes of having such a school music concert seemed to be to provide an opportunity for social bonding which will be helpful in students' future lives. In England, on the other hand, school music concerts tend to be for pupils who have chosen, or been selected, to take part. Only these pupils spend their time at rehearsals, which are usually outside normal lesson time.

I still remember that I often got bored during music lessons at school because I had been taking private music lessons outside of school from an early age. Yet I was asked to do exactly the same tasks as the less advanced pupils in the lessons. Now I know that lessons without differentiation are not an effective learning approach for individual pupils. I really enjoy applying differentiation in my lessons, as each pupil can achieve outcomes appropriate to their ability. I believe that to share differentiated tasks and outcomes with pupils in music lessons clearly helps them to set up targets by themselves for their next lesson. Having to allow for differentiation in lesson planning has inspired me to be more flexible in my teaching, carefully considering the pupils' individual learning processes.

Facilities

Can you believe that it is not common to use interactive boards at schools in Japan, even though Japan is one of the countries in the world with the highest usage of technology? Many teachers in England whom I met during my PGCE were surprised to hear this, while I was a bit embarrassed that the use of technology in Japanese schools lagged behind that in English schools. Japanese schools tend to provide only a few interactive boards, and these are for ICT rooms or multi-purpose rooms, not for main classrooms or music rooms. Digital textbooks are gradually being introduced into schools in Japan, but they tend to be used mainly for core subjects. More surprisingly, schools in Japan do not have a SIM system, so teachers register their information only on paper.

Music rooms in Japan rely heavily on old-fashioned equipment such as blackboards, CDs and DVDs. It would be very rare to use music software in music lessons. For instance, I had never used music software at primary or secondary school and had just started to use Sibelius software when I was a Masters student in Japan. I first saw and used music software such as GarageBand, Cubase, and Logic during my PGCE in England. Software such as this would only be used by students majoring in composition at university-level in Japan. This is because music education in Japan tends to deal with more traditional music. Each pupil typically needs to buy a melodica, a soprano recorder, or an alto recorder for music lessons at school. In other words, pupils in Japan are always surrounded by instruments such as pianos and percussion instruments in their music room and they tend not to have music technology equipment such as music software and recording studios in music rooms.

I think it is a real advantage that music facilities in English schools include music software and recording equipment. Interactive boards are also common at schools in England, and even in music rooms they are sometimes seen in addition to white boards. Such music facilities vary depending on the school, but the music facilities in England are far ahead of those in Japan. Therefore, I feel that music teachers in England are required to have a wider range of skills in order to use online resources such as YouTube and music websites when delivering music lessons. The use of ICT in music lessons became one of my strengths during my PGCE training. I like to search for useful music websites and media online and I am amazed at the enormous number of online music resources in English. As a music supply teacher in England, I have become more flexible in my use of music facilities in different schools. I believe that pupils can be highly motivated by teachers who can make effective use of ICT resources. I hope music teachers in Japan can soon incorporate such resources in their lessons, and have access to music facilities with better and more electronic capability. It would surely help suit the needs of music education as we move into the 21st century.

Music textbooks

Schools in Japan follow music textbooks based on the Course of Study approved by the Japanese Ministry of Education (MEXT, 2008a,b). It is mandatory for every Japanese school to follow the guidelines of the Course of Study. Music textbooks and supplementary resources, such as workbooks, CDs and DVDs based on the Course of Study, are produced by several educational publishers. Music teachers can choose and use these published supplements in addition to creating their own original teaching materials. Each school or local authority is allowed to decide which series of music textbooks is most appropriate for its pupils. The music textbooks of a Japanese educational company called *Kyo-gei* are an example of such a series. *Kyo-gei* publishes a general music textbook for each year group from Grade 1 to Grade 6 at the primary level (Kyo-gei, 2012a). At the secondary level (ages 12–18), music textbooks by *Kyo-gei* consist of two categories: general music books including singing, creative music-making and appreciation activities; and instrumental music textbooks where the music includes Japanese traditional instruments (Kyo-gei, 2012b).

By contrast, at KS1–3 in England, music teachers can decide what materials suit pupils in each school, though KS4–5 music tends to follow closely the syllabus of the GCSE and A-level examination board chosen by each school. At each school I have taught in, I have seen original schemes of work and booklets created by music teachers being used alongside published music textbooks. I think that English teachers are keener than Japanese teachers to develop a wide range of music resources sharing their ideas. Although music teachers in Japan are very keen to develop their effectiveness in using particular music activities in a given textbook, opportunities to develop their own music materials are limited by the legal requirement to use the published music textbooks. During my PGCE, I spent a lot of time creating original PowerPoint slides and worksheets for my music lessons which helped me improve my ability to devise music teaching materials.

An interesting point of difference is that music textbooks in Japan tend to categorize activities according to the elements of music, while those in England are mainly categorized by genre. For example, the music learning map in the index of the junior high school Grade 1 general music textbook (Hatanaka et al., 2011) shows which music focuses on learning which element of music, grouping them according to elements such as timbre, texture, harmony and rhythm. On the other hand, for instance, music overviews at KS3 at my PGCE school placements in England are described by style, genre or tradition, such as medieval music, pop music and blues. During my PGCE, medieval music was a type of music which I had never taught in Japan, so I really struggled to create my own scheme of work. There were other musical styles and genres which I taught for the first time here such as pop music, graphic scores and minimalism. As a Japanese person, I am sorry to admit that the music curriculum in England covers a wider range of genres and draws from a wider range of cultural contexts, including European and Asian countries. The music curriculum in Japan has a limited range of music, including some focus on Japanese traditional music such as Koto and Shakuhachi.

Another interesting point is that Japanese music education includes Japanese traditional music in the textbooks, as regulated by the following excerpt from the Course of Study:

> With regard to instruction on Japanese instruments, efforts should be made so that the students can experience the value of traditional music of Japan and the local area through music-making activities for one or more types of instruments over the three grades. (Monbusyo, 1999b: III)

Based on the Course of Study, at least one Japanese traditional instrument must be taught in junior high school. There is no comparable requirement for English traditional music in the National Curriculum in the England. It might be complicated to teach only English traditional music, because in England there are many pupils from different countries and the teachers would need to equally respect and deal with each traditional culture in their music lessons. However, I feel that it might be worthwhile to teach original traditional music of various countries so that pupils can understand the music culture of their native country as well as where they live.

In summary, there is much more freedom to select music resources in England than in Japan. However, to deliver music lessons using an appropriate selection of music resources depends on the ability of each music teacher. By having had to search for useful music teaching materials from books or online, my music knowledge has improved greatly and I am much more able to teach a wide range of music genres without music textbooks.

Transition

I think that it might be appropriate to make one other observation: namely that it is important to have more careful transition or coordination between key stages in England, especially from KS2 to KS3, in order to let pupils gradually develop their music skills year by year. In Year 7 music lessons at my school placement, there were some pupils who had not received proper music education at primary school, while there were others with excellent music skills, due to their primary school music lessons having been taken with music specialists. In contrast, music teachers both at primary level and secondary level in Japan clearly know the contents of each level of music education, as Japanese music education is dominated by the content of specific music textbooks. I would like to be a music teacher in England who understands music both at the primary and secondary levels and who is keen to develop the strategies to support smooth transitions for pupils.

The future

It is possible to understand music education systems in different countries, but it is much more demanding to understand the cultural context in which those systems have developed. This is also what I felt when I had completed my Masters thesis. Am I a real music teacher in England? I cannot teach music like a British music teacher due to my lack of understanding of some aspects of British culture. I always need to teach music without hiding my Japanese nationality, as it is the best way to express myself as a music teacher. I cannot change the fact that my music teaching knowledge and skills were developed both in Japan and in England.

It has been important for me as a music teacher in England to understand that cultural differences lead to different methods and goals for music education in England and in Japan. I am striving to adapt to different school contexts and to explore and develop my own approach to teaching music. More flexibility in, for example, lesson planning and delivery, and the acquisition of 'more advanced music knowledge and skills' are my crucial targets to be a better music teacher in England. I strongly believe that there is no fixed music teaching ability which can be used throughout the world during my entire career. My knowledge and abilities will need to evolve as I continue working as a music teacher. One thing that has really impressed me as I have worked with more experienced teachers in England during my PGCE, as well as my current supply work, is that they are very keen to develop new educational approaches such as computer-based music lessons, including the use of interactive boards and music software. I think that such an attitude on the part of more experienced teachers is necessary to develop music education which meets the needs of internationalization in music nowadays.

With the development of the digital music industry in the 21st century, music education may grow more rapidly and widely than in the last century. I believe that we as music teachers will need to maintain a good balance between digital music and traditional music. Furthermore, we will need to understand music from different traditions in more depth, so that pupils can fully understand music in different cultural contexts. One of my targets during my second phase as a qualified music teacher is to explore more effective music teaching approaches based on educational developments in the 21st century. Then, my dream for the future is to put myself into an international school environment where I can explore more deeply music education in different cultural contexts. I hope that I can be a music teacher who helps pupils understand the world's wide variety of music, together with its cultural background, and who can encourage the lifelong enrichment of their lives with music.

References

Benzil, P. S. et al., (1997) *Essential Learners Outcomes for the Fine Arts.* Maryland: State Department of Education.

Cooper, F. et al., (2000) *General Music Curriculum Guide Grades K-5 Division of Instruction Department of Curriculum and Instruction.* Charles County: Board of Education.

DfEE (Department for Education and Employment) (1999) *National Curriculum for England: Music.* London, DfEE Retrieved May 20, 2012, from www.education.gov.uk/schools/teachingandlearning/curriculum/primary/b00199150/music.

Department for Education (n.d.) *National Curriculum Music Key Stage 3.*

Hatanaka, R. et al. (2011) *Junior high school Grade 1 general music textbook*, Japan: Kyo-gei.

Kyo-gei (2012a) *Japanese primary school music textbook lists.* Retrieved May 20, 2012, from www.kyogei.co.jp/publication/textbook/h23_elementary_school/index.html.

Kyo-gei (2012b) *Japanese junior high school music textbook lists.* Retrieved May 20, 2012, from www.kyogei.co.jp/publication/textbook/jr_high_school.html.

Mahlmann, J. et al. (1994) *National Standards for Arts Education*. MENC.

MEXT (Ministry of Education, Culture, Sports, Science and Technology in Japan) (2008a) (n.d.) *Japanese Course of Study: Music for Primary school*. Retrieved May 20, 2012, from www.mext.go.jp/component/a_menu/education/micro_detail/__icsFiles/afieldfile/2009/04/21/1261037_7.pdf.

MEXT, Ministry of Education, Culture, Sports, Science and Technology in Japan (2008b) *Japanese Course of Study Music for Junior high school*. Retrieved May 20, 2012, from www.mext.go.jp/component/a_menu/education/micro_detail/__icsFiles/afieldfile/2011/04/11/1298356_6.pdf.

Monbusyo, The Ministry of Education, (1999a) *Shogakko Gakushu Shido Yoryo Kaisetsu Ongaku (Japanese Course of Study Music for Primary school Handbook)*. Japan: Kyo-gei.

Monbusyo, The Ministry of Education, (1999b) *Chugakko Gakushu Shido Yoryo Kaisetsu Ongaku (Japanese Course of Study Music for Junior high school Handbook)*. Japan: Kyo-gei.

Ogusu, T. (2005) *A study of Music Standards in Maryland, USA with a focus on Primary Music Education in Charles County*. Unpublished Masters thesis, Tokyo: Gakugei University.

QCA (Qualifications and Curriculum Authority) (2007) *Music: Programme of Study, Key Stage 3*. London, QCA. Retrieved May 20, 2012, from www.education.gov.uk/schools/teachingandlearning/curriculum/secondary/b00199601/music.

'It's revolutionary!': a case of interdisciplinarity in music education

Eric Shieh

> Why are teachers not permitted, indeed, encouraged, to show students that academic knowledge is not self-contained, that it often reaches out toward and back from life as human beings live it? (Pinar, 2004: 186).

It is a Wednesday evening and our entire seventh grade teaching staff has been sitting around a table for four hours, deliberating what it is we wish students (aged 12–13) to understand about revolutions. Are the richest explorations to be found in questions of why people revolt? Or perhaps it is a personal matter about how we each change our minds? We argue passionately. At times we are funny. I make a (half-facetious) attempt to convince the team that Marxism ought to be our defining lens, and all the work for our seventh grade in the next three months should be based on an analysis of class struggle. This is not entirely dismissed. We push, listen, refuse to budge, and finally agree. In the end, we decide that, for these next three months, we will ground our curriculum in the question of how big changes are made, and in particular how and why ideas spread.

When I say we will ground our curriculum, I mean this: all twelve teachers in the seventh grade, regardless of discipline, will address the question 'What does it take to make big change?' over the next three months. We will address it in a myriad of ways, from an exploration of the role of print media leading up to the American Revolutionary War to the role of blues songs in developing radical consciousness in black Americans — but we will all anchor to it, class by class, month by month. This whole-school commitment to a comprehensive kind of interdisciplinarity, where all courses in each grade bind themselves to a very limited number of guiding questions at any given time, often surprises visitors to our school. It also surprises visitors that by the end of the three months, seventh-grade students will have run their own media campaign to advocate for alternative engine designs for New York City taxis, and that they have done this in partnership with the New York City Taxi and Limousine Commission. The commitment, and this outcome, I would argue, come from the same place. But I get ahead of myself.

My project here is to describe, in theory and in practice, a large-scale curricular experiment I have helped to start in New York City — an experiment that takes place at a state school founded two years ago, and that is marked by its interdisciplinarity. I will outline the curriculum process, share its reasons and outcomes, and supply snapshots of the music curriculum as it has developed thus far.

The big ideas

It goes without saying that interdisciplinarity does not justify itself as its own achievement. The joining of various disciplines in a particular instance — what commonly passes for interdisciplinary work — itself is useless if there is no reasoning behind it. The opposite is similarly true: the separation of disciplines is empty without reasoning behind it. Nonetheless, a number of reasons are generally offered, if only in retrospect, and have served schools well: interdisciplinary work is often truer to real life, it creates more opportunities for students to see patterns between disciplines when constructing knowledge, it provides students greater opportunities to make personal connections, or it allows students of different strengths to find ways into curriculum (Beane, 1997: 16–17; Wood, 2005: 5–9). These are important reasons.

Primary among the reasons for my school is the commitment to what we call big ideas — the ideas that we as educators believe our students must grapple with as they grow into citizens of this world — what Beane (1995: 616) has called 'self and social meanings'. For example, some of the ideas we have used these past two years to drive curriculum include the idea of what makes a city livable, which stories we choose to tell about ourselves as a nation, and what we do when we encounter the new. It is a commitment to schooling as something anchored to the world and to our lives, athwart an educational landscape that seems to have forgotten both. Indeed, our commitment to this kind of understanding is explicit in the name of our school: the Metropolitan Expeditionary Learning School (MELS), 'A School for a Sustainable City.' The tagline specifically names our school as a site of intervention, where curriculum responds to place. We exist in and act upon New York City, from its economic to its environmental practices — an aspirational commitment rich enough, I believe, to encompass and give direction to much if not all of the knowledge and skills we might ask of our students.

For many teachers, ideas of the self and the social are generally perceived as the purview of Social Studies or Humanities classes, I suspect because that is where they have traditionally been addressed. But my colleagues and I would argue that to engage in any of the ideas I have named requires the building of knowledge and skills across multiple disciplines, and that all disciplines can benefit from their engagement. To return to the example of the curricular unit (called an 'expedition' at my school) on revolutions, the big idea of how large-scale change happens requires investigation of multiple kinds of revolutions. An understanding of not simply historical and political ones, but also technological and social revolutions, is necessary to grapple with the ways change occurs in society, and the different possibilities through which revolutions might emerge. In the year 2012, this expedition must also include a study of media in the proliferation of ideas — a study that belongs as much to music as any other discipline. Which is to claim that in order to effectively comprehend the idea of revolution, and apply that knowledge to their own contexts as agents of change, students must participate in interdisciplinary study. Big ideas demand it.

As a music educator, the commitment to big ideas excites. It activates my personal commitments as an educator and human being, and allows me to realize my craft in a way that is not reduced to the narrow teaching of performance skill. Musical contexts that were once secondary in my work as a former orchestra teacher now take centre stage: how sound constructs space (in the expedition on livable cities), how race defines our attachments to particular kinds of music (in an expedition on origin narratives), how we approach music that is new and, consequently, how we approach the works of others (in an expedition on encountering the new). Such big ideas in music are ideas I believe all responsible participants in any music culture must now grapple with.

In my school, the creation of big ideas, and the guiding questions that drive them, mark the first step in curriculum planning. As my opening vignette might suggest, time and space for teacher collaboration is imperative: all teachers in a grade team at MELS meet several hours each week for the sole purpose of curriculum design. It is in grade teams that we build capacity as a team for what we believe is important to teach, and — just as important — how we individually and collectively apprehend the big ideas. We begin with a topic we have laid out at the beginning of the year (e.g. revolutions), and proceed to brainstorm and forge consensus around two or sometimes three big ideas. As we evaluate and test the topics and ideas, below are some of the questions we ask:

- Is the idea engaging to students? Is it emotive?
- Does it address issues that are relevant to our community and world?
- Does it provide opportunities for in-depth, student-driven investigation?
- Does it hold an element of controversy? Does it allow students to consider multiple perspectives?
- Does it require students to engage in complex thinking?[1]

It is worth noting that this process of starting with big ideas differs from many common approaches to curriculum design, which often begin with a set of standards and move logically to outcomes, assessments, and learning experiences (cf. Wiggins & McTighe, 2005). At MELS — and I would argue in real life — we choose to begin with more than state standards. We do not attempt to streamline the fact that schools stand at the intersection of so much more: society's aspirations, student experiences, a specific community with its own needs, teacher expertise. I believe deeply that a curriculum requires multiple starting places, and that the best curriculum begins in a discussion of what they might be.

In disciplines: an expanded musical space

After the big ideas and guiding questions are agreed upon, the second step is for individual teachers to outline possibilities for their disciplines. In music, I ask what content and skills will allow students to enter musically into the guiding questions, develop performance skills (I teach instrumental music), and also meet the music standards for the state of New York. It is here that standards, too isolated for the discussions over big ideas, find their place.

To return to the example of revolutions and 'What does it take to make big change?', one musical possibility was immediate: an exploration of the blues. The blues both changed the landscape of American popular music through the introduction of the backbeat and blues notes, and provided a means through which black Americans articulated struggle and found agency in the articulation. Using the line '. . . and I can't be satisfied' from B. B. King's 'Three O'Clock Blues' as a jumping-off point, I created the first of two musical case studies, or projects, for the expedition on revolutions. Seventh-grade music students would compose and record blues songs over pre-recorded back-up tracks. The skills that students would meet in instrumental music included: new notes via the G and D blues scales, basic improvisation on the blues scale, and song composition in the creation of melodies for blues lyrics. Just as important, students would come to understand the blues not simply (or even immediately) as aesthetic form, but fundamentally as social response leading to social change.

At MELS we speak of two kinds of interdisciplinary connections. The first are loose connections—the connections all disciplines share in grounding curriculum in a small set of big ideas at any given time. The second are tight connections, which develop when a particular case study proposed in one discipline can share a project with a second. In this case, when I bring my proposed case study entitled '. . . and I can't be satisfied' to the seventh grade team, the English teachers immediately suggest that students write the blues songs from the perspectives of characters in their book club books—characters in books such as *Red Scarf Girl* and *Persepolis* that are caught up in revolutionary times. The lyrics would be an assessment of students' use of figurative language, as well as their understanding of the blues as an articulation of struggle. For a month of the case study, I would teach a joint project with English teachers, with integrated daily lesson plans.

A second tight connection arrived via social studies, where teachers proposed a case study on the spread of revolutionary ideas during the American Revolutionary War via print media, including pamphlets and newspapers. I immediately noted that the Revolutionary War period provided the U.S. with a rich wellspring of popular songs, from 'Yankee Doodle' to 'Revolutionary Tea'—many of which are tricky to interpret and also revealing of the period. The social studies teachers agreed to add songs to the list of media, and together we developed a project where students would analyze the lyrics from the period, making inferences on their potential value in creating change. Additionally, students would learn two-part instrumental arrangements of these songs in partner-groups—developing required skills in interdependent playing and dotted crotchet rhythms.

Given these two case studies, a guiding question for music during the entire expedition became: 'How do songs contribute to big change?'—an important and challenging question for all musicians to wrestle with. By the end of the expedition, all students were able to answer the question in depth, with reference to multiple kinds of songs. Just as importantly, students would not look at songs (and certainly not the falsely innocuous veneer of mass-produced pop songs) the same way again. This in addition to meeting several state standards for seventh-grade curriculum in instrumental music.

Physical Education	Social Studies	Music	English	Mathematics	Science
Kenneth Cooper Students apply concepts and principles of Cooper's training to improve fitness and understand that health and fitness can lead to self confidence and empowerment.	**'Join or Die'** Students explore various forms of media leading up to the U.S. Revolutionary War, including songs, pamphlets, newspapers, and cartoons. Using historical information on the growth of the colonies and the developing relationship with Britain, students contextualize and infer the effects of these works. In music, students learn duet arrangements of various songs (including 'Yankee Doodle', 'Revolutionary Tea', 'Johnny's Gone for a Soldier', 'God Save the 13 States', 'Chester').		**What is a Revolution?** Students explore perspective and bias in reading book club books about different revolutions (ex. *Persepolis*, *Red Scarf Girl*, *The Red Umbrella*).	**If the World Were a Class of 30** Students scale statistics about global issues to a personal context, and use various graphic representations of data in an effort to mobilize people to their particular causes.	**How Did They Do That: Flying in a Balloon?** Students study transformation of matter and conservation of energy in the design of hot-air balloons. **Combustion Engines: The Need for Speed** Students study chemical changes via combustion engines and the opportunities and obstacles engines created for society.
Soccer Students explore soccer's growth as a community sport, and its implications for fitness physically and psychologically. Students develop a personal fitness plan.	**3/5 of a Person?!** Students study the achievements and limitations of the constitution through the lens of its compromises.	**...and I Can't Be Satisfied** In music, students examine the blues as a particular song form that has played a critical role in the reshaping of American music and revolutionary consciousness. In English, students create blues lyrics from the perspective of a character in their book club book, which will be set as a blues melody. Following lyric creation, students in English will write "bias essays" based on a revolution topic of their choice, and researching across multiple perspectives.		**Green Taxis 2013** Students build fuel cells in collaboration with Cooper Union School of Engineering, and study how fuel cell and hybrid cars work with respect to engine design. Students use rates of change to evaluate different engine designs that are currently being considered for NYC taxis in terms of energy consumption and pollution emissions.	

Culminating Product

Students design an ad campaign based on their findings from Green Taxis 2013, and carry it out with the extended school community (including family and friends). A group of students present their findings to the NYC Taxi and Limousine Commission's Board of Directors.

Table 1. Seventh Grade 'It's Revolutionary' Expedition 2011–2012: Case Studies Map

In Table 1, above, I've included a snapshot of the entire expedition entitled 'It's Revolutionary' for the 2011–2012 school year. Each column represents a different discipline with individual case studies and brief descriptions included in the column. Note that the expedition is somewhat unusual because both of music's case studies represent 'tight' connections with other subjects.

Enactment: new teachers, new students

What does this model ask of teachers, and in particular music teachers? In the United States, where most secondary music teachers (myself included) are trained to conduct orchestras, bands, and choirs, how can educators be asked to teach the blues for several months? To teach the musicological work of making inferences based on historical songs? It means that music educators must be more than skilled musicians, and must bring a broader understanding of music to bear in the classroom. It means that music educators must bring more of *themselves*, as agents of curriculum design. It is no accident that for me the blues have taken a central place in this particular curriculum: blues and its role in shaping American consciousness has been a research interest of mine since college. Other music teachers might find different topics compelling to teach. On the other hand, this curriculum has indeed pushed my own musical capabilities: for the improvisation work I brought in guest jazz musicians to assist my teaching for the first year, and I was only able to teach the songs of the American Revolutionary War after significant independent research.

Independent research isn't the only requirement for developing a curriculum where sometimes the best curricular choices fall outside one's expertise. There is also the issue of collaboration. For the blues-song collaboration between English and music classes, I needed to read the three books students chose from for their book clubs in order to effectively aid in the assessment of the lyrics; I created the rubric on figurative language and perspective jointly with my English colleagues.

But the payoff is this: when the students realize that English class and music class are effectively merging for a few weeks, there is palpable excitement from students who are eager for what promises to be an epic project. Occasionally there is a groan or two: 'But I haven't read my book!' exclaims Jeremy, for example. In response, I sit down with him, 'Well you'd better start.' He looks at me and realizes that he's not about to fail two classes, and particularly not one in which he is used to excelling (music). There are also students who typically struggle with music class that now have an entry point to this project — the writing of lyrics in English class — and a renewed sense of possibility for their work.

The payoff is also this: a collaboration with the New York Taxi and Limousine Commission in which students evaluate different kinds of engines under consideration for the building of 'greener' taxis, and present those evaluations to the Commission's Board of Directors. And thanks to the investigations into various forms of media in all classes, and in-depth study on how perspectives are represented in narratives and graphs, it is now possible for students to devise their own ad campaign in support of their evaluations. Thus, while the case study 'Green Taxis 2013' explicitly belongs to science and maths, the final ad campaign project clearly grows out of all six disciplines and is supported by all disciplines. Such projects are a regularity at MELS — they happen in each grade, three times a year at the conclusion of each expedition. At least once in each grade, music serves as the prominent discipline for a culminating project. Students look forward to these projects as a synthesis of the work of most, if not all of their classes, and a place where their work is brought to bear on the surrounding communities or city. In this expedition, they truly explore the question 'What does it take to make big change?' as citizen-scholars.

Let me be honest: the work is hard, and even in our second year many expeditions do not find culminations that are appropriately 'epic' (to use one of our students' favourite words) — we are still working on them. This kind of curriculum design requires all educators to buy into building their own capacities in multiple directions, and many of us struggle to balance the demand for connection with the responsibility for a rigorous curriculum as we grow beyond the ways we were taught. Few case studies look like the simple learning of orchestral music that I am familiar with, culminating in an orchestral performances (in fact, only one out of the 15 case studies I have designed in grades 6–8 is concerned with this). Time and resources for collaboration also pose a challenge: a large portion of our school budget goes to hiring additional teachers (compared to other U.S. schools) so teachers can teach fewer classes, and to paying for additional collaboration time after school. Barring an extraordinary change in funding for state schools in the U.S., this will grow increasingly more difficult as our school grows over the next four years. How we do more with less — more teachers, more students, and less funding and time — is a question that currently worries us. Certainly it is an interdisciplinary question.

Conclusion

> Do we have the broad social and political will to ask what it means to be human with all of our students? I do not believe, today, that we do — at least not with all of our students. (Seidel, 2012).

When I first began teaching, I understood interdisciplinarity to mean the act of tying another discipline to my classroom. In most cases, my interdisciplinary work included some nod to maths or writing; once we read a book in music class and another time I taught rhythms using fractions (never mind that students had learned fractions in their maths class two years before). If I were lucky, it would include collaboration with another teacher — more often than not with another arts teacher — and lead to something like a musical production.

But I would argue, and have tried to describe here, that the push toward the interdisciplinary should neither rest in collaboration, nor in the integrating of disciplines — though both are central. The push to the interdisciplinary is the push to teach the world first, and then to ask music's place second. It is to recover the responsibility of education to educate for citizenship, to educate for a more just public sphere — and trust that there is a place for music. Of late, there has been much discussion in the music education profession regarding authenticity in the music classroom: what is authentic music-making? Authentic music-learning? Music that is authentic to students' lives? (cf. Allsup, Westerlund & Shieh, 2012). Perhaps another way of looking at the issue is to ask how, authentically, we might teach the world;

how we might engage in an education that asks, foremost, what it means to be human with all of our students, and secondarily find how music — to use a formulation by Elizabeth Gould (2009: xiii) — 'might matter'.

In my two years working at MELS, I have sometimes found myself afraid that music might be lost, that it may be eclipsed by other disciplines or forced into engagements considered extra-musical by most music educators and certainly state and national music standards. Sometimes I am afraid that it may not matter, that when a grade team has settled on its big ideas, I may find music has nothing to contribute. But to my surprise it emerges, again and again, in new forms and new explorations, for myself and for my students.

Acknowledgement

I am indebted to the following team of teachers who have allowed me to share our collective work: Robin Baumgarten and Anastasia McLetchie (English language arts), Matthew Brownstein and Hilary Rosenfield (social studies), Emily Edwards (special education — English, social studies, mathematics), Shayna Garrison (physical education), Paco Hanlon and Bennie Lee (mathematics), Abigail Sewall and Jenna-Lyn Zaino (science), Susan Shiney (special education — science).

References

Allsup, R. E., Westerlund, H., & Shieh, E. (2012) Youth culture and secondary education. In G. McPherson & G. Welch (eds.), *The Oxford handbook of music education*. London: Oxford University Press.

Beane, J. (1995) 'Curriculum integration and the disciplines of knowledge.' *Phi Delta Kappan,* 76(8), 616–622. Bloomington, IN: Phi Delta Kappa International.

Beane, J. (1997) *Curriculum integration: Designing the core of democratic education*. New York, NY: Teachers College Press.

Expeditionary Learning Outward Bound (2011) *Expeditionary learning core practices: A vision for improving schools*. New York, NY: Expeditionary Learning Outward Bound.

Gould, E. (2009) Introduction. In E. Gould, J. Countryman, C. Morton, & L. S. Rose (eds.), *Exploring social justice: How music might matter* (xi–xvi). Toronto, ON: Canadian Music Educators' Association.

Pinar, W. (2004) *What is curriculum theory?* Mahwah, NJ: Lawrence Erlbaum Associates, Inc.

Seidel, S. (2012, April) Keynote address presented at the Expeditionary Learning National Conference, Denver, CO. Retrieved from http://vimeo.com/channels/elnc/42222209 June 2012.

Wiggins, G. & McTighe, J. (2005) *Understanding by design* (2nd ed.). Alexandria, VA: Association for Supervision and Curriculum Development.

Wood, K. (2005) *Interdisciplinary instruction: A practical guide for elementary and middle school teachers* (3rd ed.). Upper Saddle River, N.J.: Prentice Hall.

Endnotes

[1] Several of these questions are shared by other Expeditionary Learning Schools in the United States—a loose network of schools committed to conceptualizing curriculum as interdisciplinary and project-based. While my school's approach differs markedly from others in the network, a broad document of *Core Practices* (2011) available online through Expeditionary Learning Outward Bound provides an important resource for any educators looking to build interdisciplinary curricular units.

Becoming a metropolitan music learner

Sinae Wu

*The bird fights its way out of the egg. The egg is the
world. Who would be born must first destroy a world.*
       Hermann Hesse: Demian (1919)

For me, the process of learning music has been filled with successive experiences of 'breaking eggs'. If the whole journey can be seen as a long line, the line was made up of countless dots, which contained challenges, painful lessons and fun experiences. Where I thought I'd broken one egg, there was another bigger one already waiting for me. Each egg meant another 'world', as the German poet and author Hermann Hesse describes.

My musical identity has been shaped in three different countries. I was born and raised in Korea, studied music in Germany for over a decade, then moved to England and became a secondary school music teacher. I believe that the privilege of living in three different countries gave me an ability to see a perspective from the point of 'the other' (Georgii-Hemming, 2011: 208).

I intend to reflect on some issues in music learning based on my experiences and to give some insight into how an individual's music learning can be affected, developed and shaped through being exposed to different cultural educational settings. However, I acknowledge that each individual's music learning process is unique, regardless of cultural background, and I do not attempt to provide generalized pictures of learners in any of the three countries. In the first section, I will draw a brief biographical picture of how I learned music. The second part will discuss the status of Western classical music in Korea. In the last section, I intend to consider the role of notation based on my own experience.

My musical journey

Musical experiences are closely connected to other life experiences and conceptions (Westerlund, 1999:96). In this sense, it might be beneficial to share how I have learned music, as it can be an 'effective source of information' as to 'how musical skills are acquired within a social context' (Davidson, 2004:59).

I was born and raised in an upper-middle class family in Korea. My father was a successful professor of anthropology and my mother was a school teacher. Both of them shared the same culture — the lifestyle of Korean intellectuals, who saw European culture as the ultimate 'ideal'. They read Western European literature and philosophy, listened to Bach, Beethoven and Brahms.

Growing up in this cultural background, the only music I knew until my teenage years was Western classical music. As Borthwick's research (2000) shows, this is a good example of how parents seem to project their own musical identity onto their children. Every morning I woke up with live radio broadcasts playing Bach, Beethoven and Brahms. For me, music meant something between baroque and romantic. I was a perfect 'product of colonial music education' (Roe-Min Kok, 2011).

I started to take private piano lessons when I was four and half years old. I still remember the very first lesson, when my teacher taught me how to find middle C and D on the keyboard. At the same time, I had to learn the staff notation and by the time I entered primary school, I was able to read it without any assistance from an adult.

Primary school (age 7–12) music lessons were very boring for me. The musical activities in the classroom were of two kinds: one was the Kodály method — sol-fa singing of songs from music textbooks — and the other was playing the recorder. Most of the songs were simple Korean songs in ABA form, the majority of which were written after the Korean War. A very small part of the music textbook was made up of Korean and international folk songs. The one-hour weekly music lessons were far too long simply for singing, and the teacher got us to repeat the same songs over and over again. In those days it was common for one class teacher to manage a class of more than 60 pupils, so this kind of activity was almost an 'only option' for the teachers to control the class.

This experience made me dislike any type of singing. Many years later, when I was standing in the Berliner Philharmonie Hall singing *Carmina Burana* as a member of the university choir, or when I was singing in front of thousands of people in a Christian conference in Belfast, I still did not enjoy it.

When I was 11 years old, I had a little 'breakthrough'. I was given the job of accompanying the class singing on the organ during music lessons. My feet hurt after a while and it often I felt like a physical exercise rather than making music. As far as I remember, I never heard terms that I now think of as indicating a good quality of teaching, such as 'differentiation', 'provision for the advanced pupils' or 'encouraging creativity'. All 60 pupils were expected to do the same boring tasks. I do not know whether my peers enjoyed any of those singing tasks. I assume that no one really cared whether any of the children were taking pleasure from music-making. In most Asian cultures, children are expected to follow instructions without questioning them. They must respect whatever is happening in the classroom. For this reason, they are well disciplined, focused and hard working. I do believe that this culture has encouraged Korean people to achieve remarkable economic growth but this kind of environment can be stifling when it comes to creativity. No one really learns how to think independently. However, the situation is improving and the current curriculum, introduced gradually since 1997, is described as 'a student-oriented curriculum emphasizing individual talent, aptitude, and creativity clearly emphasizes the importance of creativity in education'. (MEST, 2012)

In the 1980s, Korea was just emerging from poverty. Consequently, schools could not provide much more than singing activities and those who wished to take 'proper' music lessons were entirely reliant on private music schools. Throughout the six years of primary school, the only musical activity that interested me was the brass band. It was run entirely with the financial support of parents, but lasted only a few months.

In middle school (age 12–15), the situation was not much better. The only difference between primary and middle school music lessons was that in the latter you learned a lot more music theory instead of recorder playing. I was accompanying the class choir and the school choir. Once I had the privilege of playing Chopin's Valse Op 64 No 2 in front of the entire school (about 2,700 students).

When I was preparing for entrance to high school, Korea was in Olympic fever. The Korean government started to promote traditional music, as they felt the need to revive their own culture and introduce it to their guests from all over the world. They had begun to realize that while they had achieved remarkable economic growth, they had lost their cultural identity.

Influenced by this policy, I started taking private lessons on the *kayagum*, a traditional stringed instrument, with prominent musicians in the field. I entered the National Traditional Music High School. This was an elite music institute with fully funded learning opportunities for only 300 students from all over the country. Just as in any other music high school in Korea, I was studying more than ten subjects (English, maths, ethics, etc.) alongside the musical curriculum, which included theory, composition, singing, harmony, sight-reading, dancing, accompaniment and orchestra. Often I struggled to find a way to devote my limited time to all the subjects as well as various music subjects.

However, my main problem was not all the subjects I had to learn. As much as I tried, I have to admit that I simply did not like traditional music at that time. I was already too far immersed in the music of Western Europe. After graduation, I changed my route and studied Western Music Theory and Composition at Seoul City University. Here I took modules such as Western music history, composition, harmony, singing, music theory (both Korean and Western), cultural studies and liberal arts.

Somewhere along the line, I decided to go to Germany, to the home country of Bach. It was there that I studied musicology and harpsichord at the *Universität der Künste* (Berlin Arts University). From the beginning of the course, all the students were required to take modules in harmony, counterpoint, choral listening, analysis, etc. These *Grundkurse* (foundation courses) were meant to build a foundation for the later music analysis at graduate and Masters level in both theoretical and practical senses. They were of a much higher standard than those I had studied at Seoul City University. It was a very exciting journey, where I attained a solid understanding of music as an aesthetic object that is to be contemplated with a 'disinterested' attitude. I utterly enjoyed seminars on music history and analysing music pieces from baroque to modern.

I spent about a decade in Germany then came to England, where I had to face some difficult challenges as well as a 'breaking egg' process into another brand new culture. I joined a teacher training course in London where I was exposed to more new music activities. The most difficult one was group composition. Having only experienced individual music tuition, I was very sceptical about group composing in general. At the beginning, I found it embarrassing and perplexing to discuss intimate feelings and thoughts about music with other people, let alone composing together. However, by the end, I was feeling free from my prejudice and enjoying each session. I believe these kinds of activities expanded and nurtured my musical life. I have learned that the exchange of musical experiences between group members is a meaningful way of 'generating ideas' (Paynter, 1992: 27).

After completing my training, I enrolled on an MA Education course, where the Music Philosophy and Sociology sessions were mind-blowing. I utterly enjoyed every second of those seminars. There has been a shift in my own music philosophy. I now have a greater awareness of music as a complex phenomenon which is produced by 'humanly organized interactions' (cf. Blacking, 1974: 26) and its performance has an enactment of different values of different social groups. And these experiences have been a process of gaining 'self-understanding through other understanding' (Elliott, 1989: 164).

Music as an identity: the status of western classical music in Korea

> Human beings act towards things on the basis of the meaning that the things have for them (Blumer, 1969: 2)

The relationship between musical taste and identity formation has been widely documented. People use music as a tool for developing and negotiating their identity by associating themselves with certain genres of music (DeNora, 2000). Musical preference becomes a symbol of social belonging or even status; this can often be seen in youth culture (Tarrant et al, 2002). Here, taste can be either confirming or contradicting according to its inherent and delineated meaning (Green, 2005). Agreed preference and value will create a 'sense of community' (Hebert & Campbell, 2000). A number of writers (Green, 1997; McClary, 1987, 1991) have discussed how social phenomena (gender, hegemony, etc.) can be reflected or represented in a musical structure. Social identity theory, as developed by Henri Tajfel and others, (Tajfel, 1978) also proposes that an individual's self-esteem is established through identification with groups the individual belongs to. Individuals also 'use' music as a means of separating themselves from another and this is why people frequently speak in terms of 'our' music and 'their' music (Elliott, 1990: 148–149). Musical culture has been described as 'the sum of attitudes, customs and beliefs' that distinguishes one group of people from another (Hirsh et al., 1998: 396).

With this in mind, how did a certain type of Korean people (middle-class intellectuals) come to identify with Western classical music? To understand why this kind of cultural 'colonialism' had taken place in their lives, I will briefly outline the history of Korea.

Korea is a small peninsula located between China and Japan. The country has been invaded more than 650 times in its history. It has been a battlefield in the colonial ambitions of countries such as China, Mongolia, Russia, USA and Japan. Korea was a colony of Japan for more than 35 years (1910–1945), during which time the Korean people's identity was systematically demolished. The so-called 'Ethnic Extermination Policy' of the Japanese government attempted to destroy the ethnic and cultural roots of the Korean people. They were not allowed to use the Korean language and were even forced to adopt Japanese names. After this long and painful period, even before they started to build new infrastructures, the Korean War (1950–1953) disconnected them further from their cultural origins and also delayed the re-shaping of their collective musical and cultural identity.

As a result of these experiences, my parents' generation had lost their identity. The upper-middle class intellectuals, who made up an extremely small percentage of the whole society at that time, looked for a new ideal in the European philosophy and began to adopt Euro-American culture, which missionaries from Europe and America had brought into Korea in the 19th century. Western classical music was something that only privileged people could 'possess'—those who were not primarily concerned about their financial wellbeing. In this way, Western culture, including classical music, became a symbol of a high status in Korea, as was also the case in many other Asian countries (Roe-Min Kok, 2011). The assumption that Western music is 'better' slowly spread out, until it became a common belief among all people in Korea regardless of status, social background or age.

My father used to go to a music café in central Seoul, where young intellectuals would gather to listen to Western classical music. For most of them, this was their only access to this music, as they didn't have record players at home. These cafés existed until I was a young teenager when, with the rapid spread of technology, they disappeared. Once, my father took us to one. The listening room looked like a small concert room. People would write down the title of the music they wished to listen to, and then the DJ played the music without announcement or comment. I still remember my father sitting in a dark room, listening to Bach's unaccompanied cello suites, his eyes full of nostalgia. Only relatively privileged people, those whose financial wellbeing was secure, had access to this kind of cultural activity in the 1960s. I believe this is one of the reasons Western classical music became a symbol of a high status in Korean society.

In the light of my background, I am aware that, at least partly, I too adopted the 'superior Western attitude' (Westerlund, 1999: 94) which defines any culture outside of central Europe as being 'primitive' (Nettl, 1956). Westerlund (1999) reports that African students learn that Western music is superior to other forms of music. This is also the case in Korea.

In the last couple of decades, there have been great efforts by the Korean government and traditional musicians to revive and encourage their own cultural heritage. There has been a significant improvement in the image and the status of Korean traditional music, which now makes up about 30% of the music curriculum in Korean middle and high schools. However, the majority of Korean young people still prefer so-called K-Pop (a term that includes all genres of Korean popular music, such as pop, hip-hop, rap, rock, etc.) to Korean folk songs. This is a good example of how the 'globalization of taste' (Waters 2001: 184) is leading the young generation towards a 'univor' (DeNora, 2000: 45) musical identity. As Bell suggests, cultural styles, ideas or governmental policies will not change the music history or the taste of young people overnight. It is the change in consciousness, in values and moral reasoning that causes the change (Bell, 1974: 479).

Learning music: with or without notation?

Westerlund (1999: 99) points out that notation is the 'centre of Western music education' and an 'unquestioned learning goal' often equated with musical understanding. Clearly, musical literacy is not the 'ultimate aim' of music education (Swanwick, 1999: 56). However, inability to read notation can limit both access to and understanding of certain type of music (e.g. complex western orchestral music). Of course, I am fully aware that there are some music cultures in the world where the process of learning music takes place without any notation. As Swanwick suggests, in this kind of culture, notation can be regarded as something that hinders fluency. He takes Korean *sanjo* (a style of improvised music, which comprises a set of related pieces for solo instruments, which gradually increase the tempo and vary the rhythm) as an example of one of these cultures, where notation has 'limited or no virtue' for performers (ibid.). *Sanjo* used to be taught and handed down in a strict one-to-one master-pupil relationship without notation.

Nowadays however, ironically enough, even *sanjo* is learned through staff notation in Korea. When I took *sanjo* lessons from one of the leading *kajagum* players in Korea, I was advised to prepare the staff notation for the pieces. My teacher used to play one phrase at a time, and then I would repeat what he played with the support of the staff notation. Very often, what he played was different from what was written down. He explained that it was merely 'a matter of interpretation'. When I was practising without the teacher, I could not remember what he had played earlier. I needed to look at the staff notation, which was an incomplete resource. As Christopher Small reminds us, in this kind of improvisational music 'the finished art object barely exists' (Small, 1977: 176). Music is an activity, a process which keeps on changing. I would suggest that for this reason, the tunes should not be captured in notations, and certainly not in the form of Western staff notations. *Kayagum sanjo* was first notated in the 1960s with Western staff notation. Traditionally, the learner was not allowed to put any extra notes into the 'original' tune. However, when the master passed away, this obligation and loyalty to the original sound no longer existed, unless this was his will. The absence of the notation provided them with a sense of 'freedom'. This explains why there are about six to seven main *kajagum sanjo* 'schools' (called *rye* in Korean). *Rye* can be identified as a kind of sub-community (Small, 1987: 178) that connects people who learned from the same teacher and shared the same musical tastes. Apart from the fact that they all have almost the same structure and a couple of similar melody passages, they became completely independent pieces of music. Sometimes I wonder if it might have been more beneficial and effective not to use the notations at all.

As mentioned earlier, my very first piano lesson took place by learning to read middle C on the keyboard. This habit was challenged when I entered the National High School for Korean Traditional Music. Here I was exposed to many different types of traditional notation, while I was learning drums, flute, singing, etc. It was both exciting and challenging making music on new instruments with unknown notations. All the notations that I learned in these periods had some factors in common:

1. The music has been notated at least a couple of decades, and possibly up to hundreds of years later than the music was composed. Traditionally, all this music was initially handed down using an aural method.
2. None of the notations were precise enough to describe the fine details, such as complex rhythms, complicated ornaments, semitones, certain playing techniques, mood and atmosphere of music, etc.

This experience was the first opportunity I had to realize that a notation can function as an aid or a 'rough guide' for interpretation, rather than a 'one to one visualization' of tonal phenomena. It was a great revelation to know that notation existed, not as an end in itself, but as a 'function'. I have learned that the form and shape of notations can vary according to the effectiveness of their functional use.

Later, while I was studying musicology in Germany, I was challenged at the other extreme. The graduate modules, influenced by the Kantian idea of contemplating music as an aesthetical object, were largely based on the analysis of notated music. When I was sitting in a course covering the analysis of Bach's inventions and fugues, a professor used to tell the students repeatedly 'music notation is not only to play the music, but also to *read*'. And when he said 'read' he actually meant 'contemplate' as an art object — as if it were a picture in an exhibition! I was fascinated by this idea, and this motto opened up the world of music analysis. I began to see notation as a place where you can meet and follow the composer's ideas in a very intimate way — especially when the music was originally written in staff notation. When I look at the score of a symphony, I feel like each note is telling a story.

During two years of studying harpsichord, I learned a different form of Western notation — figured bass. In the beginning, I found it highly demanding to 'calculate' the numbers and create an improvisation with the right hand at the same time. The absence of the right hand notation made me very nervous. It was much later that I discovered the joy of improvising, although it was mostly limited to adding some extra ornaments and embellishment to the given harmony. I do believe this experience has sharpened my aural ability.

After I came to England, I tried to learn some jazz piano. For the first time in my entire life, I had an opportunity to learn music without any notation. I was surprised to discover how much brainwork, creativity and good listening skills are required in playing jazz. It was at roughly the same time that I was playing the keyboard for Sunday services in an African church in London. Most of the songs used for worship were pop, soul, rock and ballads. The majority of choir members were immigrants from Nigeria. They had never learned music notation. They learned *a cappella* style church hymns by listening. The most difficult challenge working with them was the fact that they appeared not to have the Western concept of key. A worship leader, or the pastor, simply started to sing any song at any part of the church service. As the keyboard player, I was expected to accompany the song in whatever key the person started to sing. The mixture of different experiences with and without notation has taught me how to 'flow' (Csikszentmihalyi, 1990) in both ways. I was slowly escaping the overdependence on notation.

Conclusion

My musical journey in three countries has brought about some changes in the way I approach learning music. I have started to consider music learning according to a multicultural and an intercultural perspective (O'Flynn, 2005). And here, multiculturalism is not about 'what' to learn but 'how' to. I believe the key focus of the multicultural learning must be on both 'discriminating' and 'appreciating' the differences (Elliott, 1990: 164). The former challenges learners to identify the difference itself and encourage thinking about where those differences come from. The latter is based on the idea that music learning is about self-understanding in relation to others (DfEE/QCA, 1999; Elliott, ibid.). If music is disconnected from its cultural origin, it becomes a fossil which might be well 'contemplated' but not fully 'tasted'. For this reason, in my teaching I would not choose pieces of music only for their 'sonorous, expressive and structural impact' (Swanwick, 1988: 118), but also for their diverse cultural backgrounds which reveal something about the society's 'interplay' (Merriam, 1964: 27).

We are living in a globalized world. In the past, the word 'metropolitan' symbolized something 'innovative', 'chic' and 'advanced'. Now it has become a word which indicates a general phenomenon common to all global societies. In some way or another we are all becoming metropolitan learners. Whether — and, most importantly, how — we will accept this is entirely up to each individual's choice. As far as I am concerned, I will still break some more 'eggs'.

References

Bell, D. (1974) *The coming of Post-Industrial Society: A Venture in Social Forecasting.* London: Heinemann Educational.

Blacking, J. (1974) *How Musical Is a Man?* Washington: University of Washington Press.

Blumer, H. (1969) *Symbolic Interactionism: Perspective and Method.* New Jersey: Prentice-Hall.

Borthwick, S. J. (2000) Parenting Scripts: The pattern for a child's identity as musician: A family 'script'prospective. In: R. A. R. Macdonald, D. J. Hargreaves, & D Miell (eds.) *Musical Identities.* Oxford: Oxford University Press.

Csikszentmihalyi, M. (1990) *Flow: The Psychology of Optimal Experience.* New York: Harper and Row.

Davidson, J. W. (2004) Music as social behaviour. In: E. Clarke. & N. Cook, (eds.) *Empirical Musicology: Aims, methods, prospects.* Oxford: Oxford University Press.

De Nora, T. (2000) *Music in Everyday Life.* Cambridge: Cambridge University Press.

DfEE/QCA (1999) *The National Curriculum for England: Music.* London: DfEE/QCA.

Elliott, D. J. (1989) Key Concepts in Multicultural Music Education. *International Journal of Music Education,* 13: 11–18.

Elliott, D.J. (1990) Music as Culture: Towards a multicultural concept of arts education. *Journal of Aesthetic Education,* 24(1): 147–166.

Georgii-Hemming, E. (2011) Shaping a Music Teacher Identity in Sweden. In: L. Green (ed.) *Learning, Teaching and Musical Identity.* Bloomington: Indiana University Press.

Green, L. (1997) *Music, Gender, Education.* Cambridge: Cambridge University Press.

Green, L. (2005) Musical Meaning and Social Reproduction: A case for retrieving autonomy. *Educational Philosophy and Theory*, 37(1): 77–92.

Hebert, D. G. & Campbell, P. S. (2000) Rock Music in American Schools: Positions and practices since the 1960s. *International Journal of Music Education*, 36(1): 14– 22.

Hirsh, E. D. et al. (1988) *The Dictionary of Cultural Literacy*. Boston: Houghton Mifflin.

McClary, S. (1987) *Music and Society: The politics of composition, performance, and reception*. Cambridge: Cambridge University Press.

McClary, S. (1991) *Feminine Endings: Music, Gender and Sexuality*. Minneapolis, MN: University of Minnesota Press.

Merriam, A. (1964) *The Anthropology of Music*. Evanston, IL: Northwestern University Press.

MEST (Korean Ministry of Education, Science and Technology) (2012) *Introduction: Education System: Overview*. http://english.mest.go.kr/accessed 29/05/12.

Nettl, B. (1956) *Music in Primitive Culture*. Cambridge, Mass: Harvard University Press.

O'Flynn, J. (2005) Re-appraising ideas of musicality in intercultural contexts of music education. *International Journal of Music Education,* 23(3): 191–203.

Paynter, J. (1992) *Sound & Structure*. Cambridge: Cambridge University Press.

Roe-Min Kok (2011) Music for a Postcolonial Child: Theorizing Malaysian memories. In: Green, L. (ed.) *Learning, Teaching and Musical Identity*. Bloomington: Indiana University Press.

Small, C. (1977) *Music, Society, Education*. London: Calder.

Small, C. (1987) *Music of the Common Tongue: Survival and Celebration in Afro-American Music*. London: Calder.

Swanwick, K. (1988) *Music, Mind and Education*. London, Routledge.

Swanwick, K. (1999) *Teaching Music Musically*. London: Routledge.

Tajfel, H. (ed.) (1978) *Differentiation between Social Groups: Studies in the social psychology of intergroup relations*. London: Academic Press.

Tarrant, M., North, A. C. & Hargreaves, D. J. (2002) Youth identity and music. In: R. A. R. MacDonald, D. J. Hargreaves, & D. Miell (ds.) *Musical identities*. Oxford: Oxford University Press.

Waters, M (2001) *Globalization (Second edition)*. London: Routledge.

Westerlund, H (1999) Universalism against contextual thinking in multicultural music education — Western Colonialism or pluralism? *International Journal of Music Education* 33(1): 94–103.

Young people's experiences of learning music in other countries

James Garnett

James Garnett interviewed a group of young people who had recently arrived in the UK and asked them to describe their experiences of learning music before coming here. These are extracts from their responses. Although short, we have included them here because they provide another perspective on learning music in different cultural contexts.

Imram Vir, age 12, North India

At the Gurudwara (Sikh temple) in India I learned how to play harmonium, tabla and other things as well. Most of all the best things about Gurudwara is that the song we sing is related to God. So, we get more close to God by singing Sahabid (Singing of God). We didn't have any notes or other things we just have to work it out by the Singing of God and how to get used to this type of music in year [sic — 'in the ear' perhaps?]. I have been doing this for about ten years because I came to England in February 2010. So it is only two years since I came here to England.

Aditya, age 12, South India

In Southern India I learnt playing the keyboard. So first my teacher showed me the basics of playing the keyboard and when I got how to do it, then he gives me to play small poems like *Twinkle, Twinkle*. Then he gives me big songs like *Titanic*. Then we learn chords and we play it. Then we play with rhythm and then we get a chance to play on stage and get a certificate.

In music lessons in school we write a song, then the teacher shows us the tune. And we sing along then we learn a new song every day then we have a test.

Yoon Ha, age 14, South Korea

In South Korea, we are learning music by using text book. The school is giving us a text book, which includes many songs, many stories about music and the methods how to use an instrument. We got a music classroom like UK. Every music lesson, we are going to there and learn everything which is in the text book. I think most good point in Korean music lesson is doing lesson by using text book. So we can see the book and we can know what are we going to learn and what we learned before. But they don't have many musical resources like UK. There is only few resources for teachers that teachers can show us how to play or how it looks like. And they are showing us many videos. Like YouTube.

Martha, age 16, Nigeria
In Nigeria we learnt music in a different way. The teacher just walk in and place different kind of music book on the table and ask us to choose the music we know how to play or sing the best. But the music is only Nigerian music not any other country music. By the end of the lesson you have to sing or play the music you have chosen.

We have different instruments in my music class, like the keyboard, drums and so on. Like me I sing in my music class. When I chose music for my GCSE I really enjoyed it.

Antoaneta, age 11, Bulgaria
Music in Bulgaria is quite similar to England as we do similar things. From a younger age you learn how to keep a steady rhythm and link together to create something that sounds nice. As you get older you start to do more book work and less practical. The good thing about music in Bulgaria is that you get a choice of what song to compose. I learnt to play the accordion and the recorder in Bulgaria.

Section 3

International collaboration

'Now I dare to sing a song with the children, even with the elder children': experiences of students and teacher educators at the International Summer School in Educating Music Teachers

Sarah Hennessy, Ellen de Vugt and Michele Biasutti

Across Europe, and beyond, there is growing concern about music education in primary schools. Many countries adopt the generalist teacher approach which should mean that teachers are trained to teach the whole curriculum; and in every country music is part of the primary curriculum. However, policy makers seem unable or unwilling to support the development of the music teaching abilities of these teachers. Concerns about literacy and numeracy standards, and political anxiety about PISA rankings (www.oecd.org/pisa/) deflect attention away from the need for a broad and balanced education. In many contexts this has led to a patchy and incoherent picture for music in primary schools: some schools have strong provision and others have almost nothing. The presence in every school of teachers who are confident and willing to teach music seems, for many countries, a distant goal. The existence of out-of-hours music schools, state or privately funded, in many countries in Europe (in fact almost all apart from the UK), may mask the problem. Policy makers will argue that there is provision if it is wanted but in most cases the offer is for traditional instrumental and theory lessons — not the breadth required by the school curriculum. Whilst teacher training programmes make a significant contribution within time and resource constraints, there is room for experimentation and collaboration to support and extend this work.

The project described here set out to do this on an international level. It was funded by the EU under the Lifelong Learning Programme (LLP) in the Intensive Programmes (IPs) initiative. The objectives for IPs allowed us to exchange views on teaching content and new curricular approaches and to test teaching methods in an international environment concerning music education in elementary schools. The specific objectives addressed in the application were:

- To improve the quality and to increase the volume of student and teaching staff mobility throughout Europe, so as to contribute to the achievement by

2012 of at least 3 million individual participants in student mobility under the Erasmus and its predecessor programmes (ERA-OpObj-1);
- To improve the quality and to increase the volume of multilateral co-operation between higher education institutions in Europe (ERA-OpObj-2)
- To facilitate the development of innovative practices in education and training at tertiary level, and their transfer, including from one participating country to others (ERA-OpObj-5)
- To support the development of innovative ICT-based content . . . pedagogies and practice for lifelong learning (ERA-OpObj-6)

http://ec.europa.eu/education/erasmus/ip_en.htm

The International Summer School in Educating Music Teachers (ISSEMT) at the Department of Philosophy, Sociology, Education and Applied Psychology at the University of Padua in Italy, was a two-week programme that brought together music teachers and other arts teachers to work with undergraduate students training to be general primary class teachers. The core team was made up of three teacher educators (the authors) from Italy, England, and the Netherlands, with further tutors from Spain, the Netherlands, Italy and England contributing specific sessions. The students were from Italy, Austria, Slovenia and the Netherlands. This project was initiated and directed by Michele Biasutti who made the initial and subsequent applications and the approach to other institutions for students and tutors to participate. As anyone who has been involved with EU projects will know, the application process, financial management and reporting requirements are very rigorous. The team was very fortunate in having a very experienced project director. Most IPs can run for 3 years and an application had to be produced for renewal each year. Both tutors' and students' travel, accommodation and meals were funded by the project (there are no fees paid to tutors), and the host institution was able to purchase specialist resources (mainly instruments) for use in the project.

The summer school took place in June 2010, 2011 and, for the last time, in 2012 and so now is a good time to look back on the results and our experiences as teachers with this programme.

The project

The teaching took place at the University of Padua. We occupied one teaching room and used (as always!) corridor spaces for group work. The programme itself took place over ten days with sessions scheduled from 9 am to 5.30 pm with breaks. The contact hours were dictated by the application so could not be adjusted but we did break up the schedule with visits to cultural sites in and around Padua (these included the Scrovegni Chapel, The Bo Palace, the Botanical Gardens and the university observatory). The middle Sunday was a day off — and for most meant a trip to Venice!

The timetable included daily singing and guitar sessions in which we gave students basic tuition, explored repertoire for the classroom and encouraged the students to teach each other — which they did. In the first year the recorder was also taught but this proved to be less successful and was dropped. The first year included a lecture almost every day but as a result of student feedback these were reduced in subsequent years so that in the final year we included four (Soundscapes; Development-based Music Education; Musical Development; Planning and Assessment). The bulk of the time was given to practical workshops exploring creative approaches to classroom music-making and skill development led by Sarah Hennessy and Ellen de Vugt. The IP Director, Michele Biasutti, led the ICT workshops which involved introducing students to the use of Audacity and giving them a group project to create a sonic accompaniment to a chosen story. In the first two years students created their own sound walks around the city. Pressure of time led to this being dropped in the last year but aspects were explored in other sessions.

Drama workshops and body percussion workshops were also included. In addition to the usual non-musical starting points for creative music-making and links with language development, we wanted to give students a more extended cross curricular experience through exploring how music could be combined with other subject areas and in this context drama worked very well. The focus of the drama was on storytelling and the relationships between sound/music and expressive communication. The body percussion was very demanding and gave the students a more skill-focused experience (we discussed with them the differences in teaching styles used).

On the final day the students, in small groups, taught the rest of us a planned lesson incorporating their own ideas and those from the course. We had initially wanted to involve children in this process but school holidays had started by mid-June so this was impossible.

The students

The students were selected from four teacher training institutions in Austria, Slovenia, The Netherlands and Italy (finding undergraduate students in the UK proved impossible, partly due to timing but also due to the training constraints). In the first year, 2010, there were 23 students, and 14 in each of the two following years. Students were expected to show an interest in music teaching, hold positive attitudes towards music and possess English language skills. There was some disagreement about whether it was important that students should be able to read music. This was included in the selection criteria sent to institutions but not all students met it. In practice we found that institutions interpreted these criteria rather differently so that one institution always selected students who were already quite skilled musicians — this caused initial bemusement but was soon resolved when these students realized that the focus was on teaching rather than expert performance. On the whole, students were confident ensemble singers and about half could play the guitar to some degree (each year we had one or two very accomplished players and singers).

There were big differences between the English skills of the students. We found ways to help the students to communicate and express themselves in English. We asked the students to work in nationality groups first and to make translations in English together in their group or to work in international groups to stimulate them to talk in English. As a teacher one must be aware that if there is no answer to a question immediately there is always a possibility that it is difficult to formulate in English. In the final year, the Italian students provided an important language link for the Slovenians, some of whom spoke Italian better than English. Of course, making music or using one of the other arts gives lots of opportunities to communicate without spoken language. The drama workshops (led by James Hennessy) proved to be a powerful way to enable students to communicate non-verbally and to be playful and creative.

Language competence proved to be a much more significant issue than musical competence not only in simply understanding and being understood, but also because those whose English skills were weaker were much more exhausted by the programme — something to be taken into account in future work of this kind. From an English perspective the presence of students from England might have created a very different dynamic in the group as a whole. Sarah commented that 'as the only native speaker of English I found myself acutely aware of my and others' use of language, and pace of speech — I often acted as a mediator in teaching situations trying to find alternative or simpler language to explain or describe things'.

Among the students, there were different levels of music teaching experience. The programme was focused on generalists teaching music and before the summer school some of the students had only had experience of teaching one music lesson while others had done a lot more. There were also differences in how the music curriculum was designed and the values given to different aspects of music. For instance, use of notation and knowledge of theory were considered very important in some countries and therefore the lack of this knowledge was sharply felt by students from those same countries, contributing to their lack of confidence. In the Netherlands and England, although many students might believe these to be important, this tends not to be reinforced in their training as teachers. Another noticeable difference was the degree to which students were used to working practically in groups, and on creative tasks. Some students commented that although they had learned about this in theory they had never had the opportunity to put it into practice. The opportunity to learn by doing and the feedback received from the tutors during workshops were both appreciated.

During the three years, we searched for ways to deal with these differences: for example by differentiating the singing and guitar teaching and using different teaching methods in workshops and lectures. The summer school programme promoted both creative and social constructivist perspectives and this made it possible to 'teach as you preach' and to deal with the differences between the individual students. Peer teaching and collaborative learning were also essential elements of the project.

As mentioned earlier, after the first year we reduced the number of lectures as it became clear to us that students wanted to experience for themselves how *to do* activities instead of *to be told how to do* them. Explaining the underlying theory of why things had to be done in a certain way was increasingly presented in handouts. In the first year we also discovered that there was too much overlap in the content of the lectures. We tried to be present at each other's lectures and workshops and although this was an intensive way of working we were able to link up with each other's material and activities and this led to a more balanced programme.

Evaluation

End-of-project evaluations each year (questionnaires and group discussions) showed that all the students found the experience rewarding. They found the working schedule very intensive and especially enjoyed the times when they worked independently in groups. They enjoyed and found useful the workshop content, the opportunities to develop their own musical skills and, importantly, the experience of living and working with students from other countries. The social aspects of the course should not be underestimated and this was sometimes an issue for the host country students who were not able to join students out-of-hours so easily (several students lived out of Padua). The visits to cultural sites and other informal socializing out of hours helped to draw the group together — reflected in the effective ways in which they collaborated on the final teaching task . . . and celebrated the end of the course with us.

In a small follow-up research, undertaken by Ellen, about the experiences of five of the Dutch students one or two years after the summer school, students talked, in phone interviews, about working with an open mind:

> *I learned to be more open to another person and not immediately judging another.* (Inge, 2010)

> *You learn from each other. You learn from the different cultures. In the Netherlands we are more concerned with the individual child and we differentiate a lot. In Austria classroom learning practice makes it possible for children to learn from each other. With this knowledge in mind I lately put some kids together to learn from each other in my own class.* (Hellen, 2011)

The questions in this follow-up research were about the use of summer school material in their own teaching; whether and how attending the summer school had contributed to their development as teachers; and how useful it had been for their personal development in building their confidence to teach music and their ability to teach for creativity.

All the students reported using summer school material in their teaching. They talked about the songs, introduction games, drama activities (using a picture book) and working with rhythms and percussion instruments in the classroom. They remembered a lot, even after two years:

> *The fact that I still know all these activities says something about how these activities made an impression on me.* (Nicole, 2010)

> *I go through my notebook now and then to find an another activity.* (Martine, 2011)

The students were asked the following question: 'How useful, in a scale from 1–10, was the attending of the summer school for you in building confidence to teach music?' (with 1 = least confident and 10 = very confident). Before they went to the summer school most of these students were not confident in teaching music (4–6). They gave a 7 or an 8 for building their confidence during and after the summer school.

In interview some of the students also talked about how they continued building their confidence after the summer school:

> *Before the summer school I always started in an unknown group of children with a lesson without any risks. But after the summer school I started with a music lesson. Other teachers reacted positive on my music lessons and asked me to teach this.* (Judith, 2011)

One of the students, Hellen, upgraded her confidence rating from 4 to 6: 'I am still a little scared to teach music'.

When asked about their personal development students again gave different answers. A few mentioned how they continued to learn to play the guitar and are using this in the classroom. But they also talked about their growing independence:

> *Before the summer school I was never on my own in a foreign country. I often think back to the solidarity I experienced with the other students.* (Nicole, 2010)

> *I normally tend to go along with the flow, to go along with developments in education that are hot. But the summer school learned me that I have to think for myself.* (Hellen, 2011)

Speaking English is one of the other things that helped them to grow personally:

> *Speaking English during the summer school made me more confident in talking in a group after the summer school.* (Judith, 2011)

Creativity and the ability to teach for creativity was a difficult question for students to answer. Initially, some of the students didn't understand the question and were saying that the summer school teachers were very creative in the way they were teaching. Even after an explanation of the difference between teaching creatively and teaching for creativity, most of the students still found it difficult to remember activities. They gave examples like making a sound story and improvising with musical instruments.

Two students said something about the educational need for teaching for creativity and how they tried to develop this in their own teaching:

> *As a student teacher I took all the musical instruments into my classroom and I gave the children the opportunity to discover sounds and music. I gave the space and freedom that were needed.* (Nicole, 2010)

> *And like I said before about extending an activity, there is more depth in my classes now. I allow my pupils to tell how to go further in an activity and I am more able to be responsive to their creativity. Because I listen and look more to the needs of the children and I adapt my teaching to pupil's everyday life, they are more interested. They learn more easy.* (Hellen, 2011)

To the question: 'What was the most useful for you?' one student answered:

> *The most important thing for me was that I discovered that teaching music is more than singing alone. There are many other musical activities to do.* (Nicole, 2010)

Most of the students answered that they now have a lot of ideas how to teach music, even without musical instruments:

> *I got many ideas about how to teach music. Now I dare to sing a song with the children, even with the elder children. Before the summer school I only started to sing if there was no other activity left to do.* (Martine, 2011)

Ellen comments: 'This summer school approach asks for a lot of interaction between the participants and as a teacher one must be sensitive to the needs of every single student. We must always ask ourselves if you listen enough. Every year is different and we cannot expect the students to react like the students of last year. We have to challenge ourselves in this.

'Doing this summer school for three years was an excellent opportunity to get experiences of all kinds. For me it was a real challenge to get involved in this summer school. In the beginning I didn't realize that it would have such an impact on my own teaching. Like the students I took home a lot of teaching material and teaching ideas to include in my own teaching. Translating my teaching content into English in order to teach in English, discussions with the other teachers and to observe others teaching made me think about the essence of my own teaching in music. Normally you don't have the opportunity to observe others and work together so intensely for two weeks without distractions of any kind.

'It was very enriching to explore the contrasts and similarities of learning situations in the different countries with the students and other teachers. I discovered that it is important to see the differences in customs and practices in primary music education and general pedagogy as a benefit rather than an obstacle for working together and this became for me one of the important messages to the students that were involved. We tried to create a programme in an environment in which students can learn from each other about music, arts and culture in Europe and about music (arts) education and education in general.'

Sarah comments: 'Through our first conversations before and during the project we found that we shared many similar views about working with generalists and working together became a real strength. Just as with school-based teachers, teacher educators can also experience isolation and may be the only music educator in the faculty (as in most countries primary generalist teacher training takes place in faculties of education whereas specialist training, outside of the UK, tends to take place in music institutions). So the opportunity to team teach and to learn from each other was invaluable. I have had the opportunity not only to reflect on my teaching but also to learn from other tutors through observing them work and especially the extended conversations we had over meals (breakfast included!).'

Michele comments: 'For me it was a very exciting experience to conduct this project and it was fantastic to work with such competent colleagues. All was easy because we understood each other at the first glance and all was smooth. During the work with the colleagues I had the opportunity to compare my views of teaching music, developing new and creative ideas in the field of music education. I developed awareness in my teaching process of educating the generalist in the primary school and about the strategies for designing and conducting the activities.

'With regard to the work with the students, the first day of each summer school was always the most stressful. It is the day in which all the students meet each other and a lot of energy was required for activating the group in a positive direction. It was considered important to create a co-operative learning environment bringing people from different backgrounds and countries together. After that it was very easy also because the music activities facilitated the process. The final day was the most rewarding for us with the planned lesson conducted by students and verifying how they applied their learning.

'I participated also in other international projects, but I think the Intensive Programme is the most interesting one, since there is a constant interaction with the colleagues in designing the activities and a direct application and contact with the students. The opportunity for working with students from different countries and with different backgrounds is also challenging, especially in the field of music education in which you can bring your country's musical traditions into the class.'

Conclusion

Planning time and good communications between the team prior to each summer school were inevitably crucial and difficult to achieve. From this and past experiences it seems that working intensively with teachers can be a better approach than the 'steady drip', when attempting to change self perceptions and to build skills for teaching. The Summer School enabled immersion and focus, and also the development of a strong, supportive peer group. Taking students, and teachers, out of their normal environment can also help them to grow in confidence.

As far as this kind of IP is concerned, our thoughts about future possibilities turn to the need for a project with a broader arts focus — perhaps a project in which students can work more independently across all the arts with more extended periods on creative projects. This would involve a rather different core team and more working spaces . . . but would be an exciting venture.

Facilitation as leadership: empowering individuals within the collective — a Soundcastle International Exchange in São Paulo, Brazil

Rachael Perrin, Jennifer Parkinson, Gail Macleod and Hannah Dunster

In January 2012 our arts collective, Soundcastle, took part in Creative Voices, an intercultural exchange in São Paulo, Brazil. We aimed to develop and share our professional skills as music workshop leaders with Brazilian music teachers and students, as well as experience Brazilian traditional music and attitudes to music-making. In this chapter we describe our experience of delivering an informal, collaborative approach to composition and music-making within the Brazilian environment of Espaço Musical, a private music school in São Paolo where most students have private instrumental and composition lessons. We reflect on the benefits of using facilitation as a form of leadership and include the perspective of Ricardo Breim, principal of Espaço Musical, who gave us feedback following the project. We focus on four aspects of the project, beginning with a summary of the background and the artists involved. This is followed by an outline of our creative approach with an emphasis on how we embrace collective creativity within a formal, educational context. Further, we reflect on the intensity of intercultural relationships and consider the social challenges and intricacies present in a project such as this. The chapter concludes with a discussion concerning the value of cultural exchange and how this can inform our professional development.

Project background: Creative Voices 2012

Creative Voices was a musical and cultural exchange between Soundcastle and Espaço Musical. Devised and managed by Brazilian musician Fernando Machado, the vision was to explore creativity and collaboration in educational settings, allowing musicians and educators to share skills, ideas and artistic voices from differing cultural perspectives.

We, as Soundcastle, specialize in creating new music through collaboration in a diverse range of contexts. As professional performers and leaders we work in settings such as community centres, schools, care homes and conservatoires, with people of all ages, backgrounds and musical abilities, as well as professional musicians and artists. Through facilitating collective music-making we aim to devise original work which reflects the creative voices of the people and the place we are working with.

Espaço Musical is a prominent music school in São Paulo, founded and directed by Ricardo Breim. The school is renowned for promoting music as a language and communication skill. Espaço Musical focuses on learning and teaching musical perception, in which learning by ear plays an important role, developing the significance and depth of the musical experience. This approach to education raises all-round musical awareness, using improvisation, composition and analysis to support performance and technique. Ricardo Breim was instrumental in writing the National Curriculum Parameters for Music (BRASIL, 1997) and was also involved in preparing the first National Examination of Students' Performance (ENADE[1]). He currently directs the Formation of Musical Educators (FME) course at Espaço Musical.

Fernando Machado is an independent musician and workshop leader from São Paulo, currently based in London. Under the name Lambrego[2] he produces, performs and records original music, taking his Brazilian influences to a wide range of contexts. In the field of education Fernando works alongside schools and community arts centres to develop creative musical work with people from differing backgrounds, promoting exchange across art forms and cultures.

In bringing together Soundcastle and Espaço Musical, Creative Voices sought to allow both parties to discover and learn from similarities and differences in their approaches, as well as to develop an awareness of their respective cultural and educational backgrounds. In terms of education, there is a large degree of separation in Brazil between the formal study of music in institutions and conservatoires, which focuses on classical and jazz genres, and the informal learning of traditional and popular styles. The legal requirement to include music in school-level education has only recently come into force in Brazil and as yet São Paulo has no system or curriculum for its implementation. However, music is embedded in the culture and informal learning can be found in all walks of life, embodying the well-loved sounds of samba and MPB (Musica Popular Brasiliera). The idea of workshop leading is fairly new and currently associated with the informal sector. From this perspective, the direction of our music education practice in London holds particular interest. Our music-making can encompass any genre, combining influences from and functioning in both formal and informal settings. The appeal of the exchange from our side is in the immersion in a culture that is inseparable from its musical identity and the exposure to the unique educational approach of Espaço Musical in this context.

Creative Voices 2012 was hosted by Espaço Musical for six days in January, and was open to staff and students at the school embracing all ages, backgrounds and musical abilities. Culminating in a performance of newly created work, the week ran in three strands, each with a different cultural and educational focus:

1. **Anglo Voices**

> Over five morning sessions, Soundcastle worked with Espaço Musical students enrolled on both instrumental and music education courses. With the overriding aim of creating new music we used models of

leadership and facilitation to explore and demonstrate approaches to spontaneous music-making and group composition.

2. Brazilian Voices

Afternoon workshops were led by Brazilian artists: Barbatuques (body percussion), Babado de Chita (traditional dance) and Ari Colares (percussion). Here we took on the role of participants and learnt about Brazilian musical traditions alongside staff and students at Espaço Musical.

3. Anglo-Brazilian Voices

During two intense creative sessions, we worked collaboratively with Espaço Musical staff. With a duel intention of devising new music and exchanging professional and artistic practice, we worked on methods of group composition and improvisation. We also held an evening discussion, which included presentations by Soundcastle and Ricardo Breim, sharing our knowledge and experience in order to develop ideas on promoting music in the community and education.

Embracing the collective

In order to lead cross-cultural workshops in Espaço Musical, we focused on collaborative composition within what is usually a more segregated educational context for individual learning. The participants were of varying ages, abilities and levels of instrumental skill. The aim was to bridge the gaps that formalized learning can inadvertently create (such as different groups for musical ability, age, instrument and musical genre) whilst simultaneously utilizing the formal, school setting to monitor the responses of all participants and encourage progression of each student's abilities. We wanted to facilitate an environment of equality, widening the students' outlook so that all felt confident to contribute. In order to achieve this, our strategy for Espaço Musical was a combination of leading, facilitating and co-leading. The following will present some brief examples of what each style of leadership entailed.

Leading

We started with a strong sense of a single leader in order to create a settled, calm environment. On the first three mornings, we began with one of us leading call-and-response singing. No verbal instructions were given once we were in the workshop space. A safe environment was created by having a clear leader and no language barrier to overcome, while simultaneously establishing group ownership of the workspace by filling it with our combined voices.

We retained a leading role for the first day during the workshop activities. However within this, we immediately encouraged the Brazilian students to take part in leading and decision-making. We were keen for participants to discover their own artistic energy; as Ken Robinson writes 'when we connect with our own energy, we are more open to the energy of other people.' Focusing on improvisation and listening exercises, the aim was to start searching for a group sound. Using hand signals to request riffs, melodies, counter melodies and dynamics, participants took turns in leading the group in structured improvisations. This enabled them to experiment with constructing a piece of music or contributing their own musical voice to the ensemble sound whilst simultaneously hearing the unique musical styles of other individuals within the group. The result was a collective subconscious awareness of the group dynamic, without the need for verbal communication.

It should be emphasized that we are careful not to use specialist language. For example, the word *improvise* was never used in the above activity. We focused instead on the idea of *play* and the impossibility of being wrong (an area to be explored more later). Following the workshop, some of our participants realized they had in fact been improvising and were surprised at their own contributions. Words such as *improvise, compose* and *perform* may carry a weight of expectation and potential failure; for instance the idea of improvising in a formal context can be intimidating. However, when interacting playfully in a supportive and safe environment where every contribution is valid, there is nothing to hold creativity back.

Facilitating

Having established a group sound and energy, we made a distinct shift from leading to facilitating. In order to exchange our cultural and musical ideas with the Brazilians we gave no more instructions and acted solely to assist the composition process, taking equal roles within the collective. Our aim at this point was 'to enable the participants to see, feel and understand the connections that are integral to the creative process.' Creating and following through ideas together in this way, the students gained a sense of ownership over not only the material but the whole process as well. The informal method enabled them to take control over their own learning, whilst the formal educational environment allowed us as facilitators to adopt a structured approach, carefully monitoring each participant's experience. Rather than composing alone or following a leader, creative energy is stimulated by the ideas of others and, in turn, the collective energy can inspire individuals to raise the bar on their own achievements. The comparison to composing alone was felt by several of the Brazilian participants:

> *The few experiences I have had previously in composition differ greatly with this one for its individual character and loneliness. The exchange of ideas provided by an experience as this was not only enriching for obtaining knowledge of music as well as self-knowledge (especially in my case, for my shyness) . . . It was amazing and gratifying to witness the contribution of each and every one, without exception, in favour of the collective, thanks to the motivation and the enabling environment provided by the instructors.*[3]

Co-leading

Following the facilitating stage, the Brazilian students were sufficiently confident to contribute ideas and guide creative processes themselves. The next step was to facilitate co-leadership, and we now actively supported participants in taking on leading roles. We encouraged students to bring their own songs, lead the daily vocal warm-ups and suggest or demonstrate ways to piece together the musical material. In the performance itself students had the opportunity to lead different sections such as melodic lines and simple dynamic developments, with some of them taking on the responsibility of opening the whole piece. At this stage effective facilitation was crucial so we were observing and guiding when needed to ensure that leadership was a combined effort, resulting in a balanced cross-cultural composition reflective of all involved.

In order for facilitation and co-leading to work, every person involved must be willing to relinquish their ego, including the facilitators themselves. One overly controlling ego in a group can isolate an individual, disrupting the dynamic and hampering the empowerment of others. As leaders we aim to ensure that our own egos do not inhibit creative processes, by avoiding a sense of controlling directorship in order to enjoy collaborative and (in this case) cross-cultural results. Following the project, Ricardo Breim commented, 'The collective creation activities are organized so that the differences in musical training and experience do not affect the symmetrical involvement of all students. In the final product, we all feel at the same time, performers, composers and improvisers.'[4]

Intercultural relationships

The nature of an intercultural exchange often means experiencing projects within an intensely condensed timeframe. In the case of Creative Voices 2012, this was six days. This intensity can advance the growth of strong relationships over a very short period of time as well as raise awareness of cultural differences in social relationships. However, it can also work negatively as a group of people under pressure can become overwhelmed or stressed as they spend an unusual amount of time together. We believe a creative approach is vital to the development of successful relationships. The foundation of our projects is to promote strong, trusting and supportive relationships between all members of the group. This is not only so that the participants feel safe to share ideas but also to encourage peer support which means that anyone struggling has many more avenues of help and encouragement. This is also helpful in mixed instrument projects where the leader does not necessarily have expertise in each instrument. In terms of building relationships, this approach prevents us as leaders from appearing separate or superior to the group. We mentioned earlier the idea of play and how within our workshops it is impossible to be wrong. Having always been advocates of this approach within our own field, it was enlightening to be recipients of it when we were out of our musical comfort zone. As part of the cultural exchange, we were introduced to traditional Brazilian dancing by the group Babado de Chita. Their leadership methods combined a gentle, warm, casual feeling with a highly positive, motivating approach. Feeling stiff and awkward compared to the fluid Brazilians, we were encouraged to follow our instincts and allow ourselves to play and explore. As a result, our fears of being judged were put aside and our bodies were freed up to experiment and push past boundaries of insecurity, feeling and expressing the rhythm of the music through movement and furthering our creative potential within the dance workshop. The session was clear evidence that our practice often has more in common with dance and drama approaches than musical ones, as the Brazilian dancers led an informal, inclusive workshop with the clear message *there is no such thing as wrong*. There are pros and cons to this within a formal context, the latter being that you can never be sure of the final product or its suitability for a particular performance. However the pros include a greater sense of achievement for individuals within the collective, the development of relationships through collective creativity and the original and unpredictable artistic material which results. Whilst there are challenges in finding a balance between leading and facilitating, this approach opens up a world of opportunity to group collaborations and empowers individuals within the collective.

Overcoming the language barrier is the most immediate challenge for many intercultural relationships. Although this can be perceived as a problem it also provides an opportunity to make music become, as Breim commented after the project's conclusion, a *'sound language of integration'*.[5] With varying degrees of familiarity with Brazilian Portuguese within the group we had to be prepared for situations in which we could not deliver or understand direct instruction. When leading, we encouraged groups to try out and demonstrate ideas rather than fall into endless discussions of what could be. The Espaço Musical philosophy made this an easy task. Students and teachers were already being trained in a different way to the usual classical instrumental approach which separates theory from practice. Their continual emphasis on learning through experience meant that the students were already used to exploring ideas through practising them rather than writing them down. An intercultural musical exchange occured very naturally in this case, as we as leaders were not teaching any musical material and individuals followed their creative instincts when contributing. Breim noted:

> as there is no prior commitment to specific musical language, the inclusion takes place also in terms of cultural differences: participants tend to propose compositional materials with which they are familiar and, as a rule, accept completely the cultural contributions that arise in the process, always taking care that the excesses or shortages do not compromise the quality of the musical result.[6]

As discussed earlier, we often use songs as a levelling device in a warm-up. These have been collected from different cultures all over the world and using simple words in a language that neither nationality is familiar with can put intercultural relationships on the same page. It became clear that the few English songs we used, though simple to us, were a little complicated for the Brazilian participants, making them nervous. Throughout the week we also experienced this in reverse when the Brazilian teachers we met moved quickly through Portuguese songs and we were unable to get a grip on the words. This gave us a new appreciation that the activity of singing together, which can be so unifying and confidence building, can also be destructive if an individual feels out of their depth. To lead and participate in workshops during the same week, although very intense, enabled us to constantly learn from and experiment with the new techniques and ideas we were observing.

We discovered that, in terms of social relationships, Britain can learn from Brazil, particularly in our attitude towards different age groups. Intergenerational practice in Espaço Musical was completely natural. All of the Creative Voices workshops had a range of participants, from age ten to people in their sixties, including some teenagers. The ease with which conversations were struck between participants of different ages and the genuine interest that people showed towards each other highlighted the lack of regular opportunity for this mixture in the UK. In Espaço Musical, it was particularly noticeable that the adults responded as equals to the young people involved. This may have to do with the fact that they were all students within a formal context, but as an overall cultural difference it was noticeable that many generations came together socially on a regular basis. The most joyous example of this was a carnival rehearsal at a local samba school. These energetic and carefree rehearsals are open to anyone and indeed everyone came, from grandmothers to toddlers and everyone in between, all joining together to sing the *samba-enredo* (the samba school's unique storyline for the carnival parade).

Professional development

Communication is currently the easiest it has ever been. We can speak to friends, colleagues and contacts in all corners of the globe without ever leaving our homes. Information is at its most accessible; Google will answer our musical queries in an instant and YouTube will bring us videos of music from around the world in seconds. So what is the value of active cultural exchange? Do we need to travel in order to truly understand the music of another culture or can we learn about it equally effectively online, saving money, energy and time?

One of the key themes of contemporary music leadership and creative music-making in the UK is learning by ear. It is common for creative projects to be delivered and received without any form of traditional notation. Also, the use of body percussion is becoming increasingly common, as is the singing of simple songs from other cultures. Being standard elements of our existing approach, these were all areas that we were keen to refresh and explore further, exchanging them with the Brazilian teachers and students and using them in formal working contexts. In order to develop a real understanding of the value of using ideas from other cultures there is no substitute for being in a country, surrounded by artists who have spent their lives absorbed in its music and culture.

To begin with, we developed many tangible, practical abilities from our exchange with the Brazilian artists. We learnt about and developed skills in body and vocal percussion, the clapping scale, Brazilian rhythms and songs and basic Brazilian dance. We have all integrated these skills into our work in the UK, both as freelance animateurs and under the Soundcastle banner. For example, we have been using the songs in our independent practice and also using ideas gained from the project as inspiration for activities in our current partnership with UK-based language school ELAC.[7] It would be unrealistic to say that during our two weeks in São Paulo we learnt to play Brazilian music; this is, of course, a lifetime's work. However we did learn extensively from the style of leadership we experienced when collaborating with Brazilian musicians. The aim of our exchange was less about the content of the workshops and more about observing and experiencing the leadership of artists who are immersed in different musical cultures. The structure of the Creative Voices exchange enabled us to demonstrate the advantages of an informal approach within a formal educational context, while in return the Brazilian artists, used to working in informal contexts, introduced us to new leadership techniques. In addition we were able to extend our musical outlook and creativity through learning traditional Brazilian rhythms and dance.

One of our primary goals is the development of intergenerational work to bridge the barrier of the age gap which is so pronounced in the UK and seemingly non-existent in Brazil. Throughout our time at Espaço Musical, it became clear that by fostering an atmosphere of listening and experimentation it is possible to build a dialogue that does not distinguish the creative voice by the age of the person. This observation was greatly encouraging for us, helping us to see how, within creative contexts and with thoughtful facilitation, different age groups can co-operate free from patronization or over-politeness.

The language barrier provided us with the perfect opportunity to explore Espaço Musical's philosophy of *musica com linguagem* ('music as language') within our own leadership practice. The latest Ofsted report makes a strong case for more music, less talk[8] and this was a motto of our time in Brazil. Using the leading, facilitating and co-leading techniques described above, we challenged and extended our own non-verbal communication skills. This has directly influenced our creative and philosophical approach, stimulating us to think deeply about the method of facilitation as leadership and how we implement it in our work in the UK. Having gained this experience and honed our skills of facilitation we were well prepared for our community project *Musical Beacons*[9] which ran in Bow and Charlton and had several social parallels with our Brazilian experiences. Participants had a wide range of musical ability and experience, and we explored the balance between leading them in the discovery of music and facilitating their ideas on how to make that music reflect their local community. Further, London's diverse cultural mix meant that many participants were also coping with the language barrier and non-verbal leading methods proved invaluable.

We aim to develop the sustainability of this exchange and are currently in conversation with Fernando Machado, our collaborator and project manager, about developing the project and returning to Espaço Musical and other interested Brazilian institutions. The evaluation feedback from the school, the participants and the team was exceptionally positive and the relationships formed and skills developed proved to us the immense value of cultural exchange to the practice of artists and facilitators.

Creative Voices 2012 taught us the benefits of practising facilitation as a form of leadership within a formal context and how it can widen the potential of cross-cultural exchange and communication. From our point of view, we were able not only to extend our practical leading skills but also to learn from Brazilian attitudes towards informal music-making, embracing groups of widely varying artistic ability and social background with high quality artistic results. Espaço Musical was able to observe and understand our implementation of informal, collaborative approaches, advancing the artistic potential of individuals within a formal educational context at a pivotal time for the development of Brazil's music education system. The artistic content of the workshops, whilst it developed and extended our own musicality, was not the primary reason that it was vital to travel to Brazil rather than conduct the exchange via the internet. In terms of professional development, the core of this project was experiencing other cultural forms of leadership. By both leading workshops and experiencing them as participants, we were constantly learning and evolving our own skills. Experiencing leadership as opposed to simply observing it or reading about it is the key to a deeper understanding of its ongoing effect on participants. There is no better way to learn this than to be a participant. Overcoming the language barrier by embodying Espaço Musical's *musica com linguagem* motto ensured that a lucrative intercultural exchange such as Creative Voices mutually benefited both nationalities, equipping us with tangible skills, philosophies and attitudes to employ in our own work as well as international partnerships to ensure that the discussion is ongoing and always developing.

References

Brasil (1997) *Parâmetros Curriculares Nacionais*. Brasília: MEC: Secretaria de Educação Fundamental.

Robinson, Ken, *The Element: How Finding Your Passion Changes Everything*, (London 2009) 94.

Renshaw, Peter, *Engaged Passions: Searches for Quality in Community Contexts*, (Delft, 2010) 69.

Endnotes

[1] Exame Nacional de Desempenho dos Estudantes, http://govbrasil.com/site-do-enade-www-inep-gov-br-enade/ (accessed August 2012)

[2] Lambrego, www.lambrego.blogspot.co.uk/ (accessed 22/07/2012)

[3] Blevio Zanon (workshop participant) Feedback during the Creative Voices 2012 evaluation process.

[4] Ricardo Breim: Reflective feedback following the Creative Voices project.

[5] Ricardo Breim: Reflective feedback following the Creative Voices project.

[6] Ricardo Breim: Reflective feedback following the Creative Voices project.

[7] ELAC (English Language and Activity Centres) www.elac.co.uk/ (accessed 22/07/2012)

[8] www.slideshare.net/Ofstednews/music-in-schools-wider-still-and-wider, Slide 6, Bullet 4. (accessed 20/07/2012)

[9] Musical Beacons: A Soundcastle community music project. For more information, visit http://soundcastle.co.uk/wordpress/?page_id=16 (accessed 22/07/2012)

Building international collaborative networks through creative professional practice

Pamela Burnard

Introduction

International collaborative networks of music educators, practitioners and researchers can show: (a) the relative importance of differing systems for learning and creating music; (b) the sensational experience of learning and creating music; (c) the diversity of practices of learning and creating music; and (d) the necessity of translating these understandings into language that can be communicated to others (Burnard, 2012).

This chapter sets out to reflect on the benefits of building networks through collaborative professional practice. These networks amplify lifelong career aspirations and assist musicians, teachers, students and researchers in the field of music education with the development of their identities. Like many teachers, I have an interest in identity, work and contemporary careers in relation to music and its teaching. I have always been fascinated by the lived experience of creativity and the influences that contribute significantly to creativity in different situations.

As a young teacher, I was curious about experiential ways of knowing, processes of creativity and the wider social and cultural values and practices that arise in different contexts. This led me to read and be inspired by cognitive theorists and by sociological and cultural perspectives that identify what distinguishes creativities in music and cultural production.

I soon began to attend regional, state and then interstate conferences where I observed and absorbed many interesting presentations. I found myself reading articles by academics and, where I could find them, practitioner researchers, I posed questions and chatted with anyone and everyone I could find who shared similar interests in these fields. More conferences afforded more opportunities for meetings (or chats over coffee) with teachers and academics. As my confidence grew, so did the opportunities. I started presenting posters at conferences. This led to the presentation of papers and joining professional networks of like-minded educators and researchers who suggested more productive ways of thinking about creativity, helping me to resolve problems relating to professional practice and research enquiry. Each occasion on which I travelled or presented a paper gave me an opportunity to widen the networks.

My intention in writing this chapter is to:

1. Demonstrate the potential of international networks for the bridging of cultures and traditions — be it between theory and practice or between

colleagues from a very wide range of professional backgrounds, countries, cultures, communities and practices in music education
2. Reflect on my journey as a musician, music educator and researcher, drawing on some of my own experiences in which I became aware of and sensitive to the benefits of building international networks in music education
3. Stimulate and encourage music teachers to develop international collaborative networks.

The case for building international networks

The forces of globalization have increased the interest in, and importance of, international trends among policy-makers, practitioners and theorists. Staying in touch with these trends is critical to improving teachers' understanding of the differences in how learners shape their identities with respect to the diversity of musical cultures and practices. To illustrate this I link two topics which, I believe, are of significant importance to music educators. Both are almost always present in any learning culture and can help to explain how music provides us with unique forms of creativity and self-knowledge and why music has an essential role in education.

The first topic concerns the potential professional benefit of developing international networks that enable music educators and practitioner researchers to build collaborations between pre-service teachers, practitioners, academics and/or other professionals. Arguably, one of the most important parts of music education — and perhaps the key to contemporary relevance — is how music teachers' professional practice relates to its cultural context. Practitioner research which illuminates teachers' national and local contexts is all the more effective when it documents classroom narratives central to understanding learning cultures. Analysing, and extending into the international arena, lines of enquiry which occupy the thinking of music teachers (such as the relationship between the world of the classroom and the world of education and policy), and understanding the impact on these of international perspectives, can help us look at music learning and teaching in relation to wider social or economic structures and power relations (including the effects of globalisation on music education).

The second topic concerns the motivational and career benefits of developing international professional exchanges — benefits which include promoting teacher reflection, broadening knowledge and participating in culturally rich dialogues. There are many debates: around whether 'diversity in practice', 'inclusion or exclusion' of music (classical, popular, or other) in formal or informal learning practices, results in authenticity in music development; about deficiencies in school music provision for the education of traditional or popular musicians; about which global policies that have impacted on schools and music education should prevail; about what the training for music should involve; about where in the world are there examples of the arts integrated at the centre of the curriculum and functioning effectively as a means of engaging children in all aspects of learning; about which non-Western nations have experienced de-colonization and dismantlement of Euro-American imperialism and how music in these nations has developed subsequently; about what has driven musicians and educators to reclaim their own indigenous identification in music; about how teachers can develop more agency as professionals; and about how to develop the agency of individual musical learners in the social structures that they inhabit.

We do not learn or teach in a cultural vacuum. As teachers, we should have no illusions about the diversity of meanings that music and music education has in diverse education systems and cultures. Central questions are: What forms of musical learning are made possible within a particular learning culture? What forms of musical learning are made difficult or indeed, impossible? Schools are meeting places for all musics. But such a meeting can sometimes result in a conflict of power, particularly in situations where the majority culture decides and shapes the content of that culture. For teachers, music education in a multicultural society is a challenge. Not everyone has the time or feels an urgent interest in how their own musical culture compares with others. This argument is clearly put by McPherson and Dunbar Hall:

> Music education based on multicultural content and teaching strategies fulfils a number of aims including the promotion of knowledge of music in specific geographical and cultural settings; the exemplification of musical concepts and processes; the demonstration of the role(s) of music in defining, maintaining and brokering culture; and the analysis of the concept of culture as a force in people's lives (McPherson and Dunbar-Hall, 2001: 23)

Culture and identity, cultural diversity, cultural education and inclusion are key concepts in the global debates about music education. In this chapter I will argue that, whether as students, student-teachers, or qualified teachers, we are more likely to experience change and the cultivation of creativity in the education field when working on exchange programmes or collaborating in joint endeavours in cross-national and international projects that involve co-ordinated partnerships between universities and schools or clusters of schools. There is plentiful evidence of how schools and teachers enhance the quality of learning for their students by adapting material from national and international collaborative research programmes (Jeffrey, 2006).

Reflecting on the pluralism of practising in diverse cultural contexts

My journey as a teacher involved in research is one of asking fundamental questions about music and creativity, about what is meant by musical creativity, and about conceptions of creativity in education and within the cultural mores in which it is experienced. I read everything I could get my hands on about improvisation and composition, both as separate measures of creative potential and as interrelated activities. I read how creativity has a catalysing effect in cultural renewal and transformation across nations, races and cultures. The premise of 'good teaching' was, I thought, what informed me as a music educator; it was what enabled me to develop pedagogic strategies to encourage and support children's musical creativity in the classroom. The idea of being innovative was of great significance to me. But I also sought to move my understanding forward in terms of looking for those intercultural and pluralistic elements in musical creativity which allow renewal and transformation.

I made contact with people who could illuminate philosophical and theoretical insights across the disciplines of psychology and sociology and related empirical research.

At this particular time in the UK there was a hugely influential Schools Council *Secondary Music Project* (1973–1982) which had promoted a widespread review of the role of composition in the classroom. Subsequently, composition (and, by association, improvisation) became centrally placed in the National Curriculum for both primary and secondary school children.

Improvisation and composition were often integrated into classroom music, but teachers had little or no understanding of how these two phenomena might be differentiated. Integral to my own understanding of musical creativity was my concern with supporting the practice of teachers; my assumptions about how children improvise and compose; and my research in terms of how the values and beliefs within our own culture influence the teaching and learning that takes place. It was these factors which shaped my approach to teaching improvisation and composition and to the key issues and concerns which informed the philosophical and political argument central to my research.

I set off on the process of interacting with people who held alternative ways of thinking about musical creativity, of how musical creativity is understood in different cultures and, most importantly, of seeking access to and researching the plurality of children and young people's views and voices. For teachers who undertake research, the experience feels unprecedented; no one has ever been just there before. It involves mixing and mingling, practising networking skills and adopting the practice of openness and receptiveness with a diverse range of people. Building support networks and intellectually supportive relationships takes time and develops in an organic and unpredictable manner. My focus was to explore children's experiences and processes of improvising and composing. To this end the reference 'into different worlds', words used by one of children in the study to describe different performance settings, relates to the study's commitment to a contextually originated, constructivist view of what children meant by improvising and composing.

What I came to understand was that although the purpose of the research was, at the time, to understand children's lived experiences by looking into the their own understanding of their experiences, I was ultimately trying to understand what musical creativity is as a vital element of the cultural process, whatever the cultural context, and to explore the way values influence the construction of teaching and learning.

Become more aware of cultural assumptions: our guiding assumptions

Travelling abroad teaches us many things. One thing becomes very clear: there is no single reality to be known, but a variety of different realities, each of which depends on the specific social, economic, cultural and historical nature of the thing under consideration. It was not until completion of the field work phase, following a move from Australia and several months settling into the English culture and environment, that I was able to stand back and appreciate exactly what I'd done. Early on in this journey, my enquiry seemed to take clear shape but the more I engaged in the research process, refining the topic and communicating the content to others, the more I felt like a person groping about in the dark, in a maze. I was an outsider researching in England. How was I to understand the role and significance of creativity and the cultural factors in the process of learning as an outsider? What were the assumptions underpinning what counts as important in the accounts of children's cultural experiences of learning and creating music?

I kept reflecting on the idea that if our aim as music educators is to have children enjoy music then we need to provide varied learning cultures and sub-identities as the core of the teacher's professional identity. I was concerned with questions such as: What role does culture play in our understanding of musical creativity? What role do global influences, especially economic, cultural and social, have in shaping our understanding of music education and musical creativity? How do we know what children know and experience of musical creativity? How do we understand children's musical creativity in relation to their cultural identity? I wanted to allow greater scope for children to construct and reconstruct their own cultural meanings of what it is to improvise and compose. I wondered if I would be able to find an approach to school music pedagogy which resonated with the children's view of themselves as musicians, performers, composers, song-writers and improvisers.

In the end, I came to learn how to access and understand children's experiences of improvising and composing and to capture, in the multiple lines of a dissertation, the 'lived situation'—where creativity, art and imagination are at the core of our work and our understanding. I learned to ensure that we do not position children passively in research contexts and that we need to listen to children in ways that faithfully represent their views, realities and experiences of musical creativity. It was no simple matter.

Final thoughts

Music reflects the values of society. Music is an important part of our identity. Culture and identity are intertwined and are the most important organizing concepts in modern society. With this insight, some of the most important educational questions of the day for music educators concern discussion of the kind of music knowledge that people can acquire at school, college or university and the assessment of this learning (i.e. what is included or excluded) as distinguished from the knowledge that people acquire in their everyday lives and in their families and community[1]. For example, folk and traditional music are extreme markers of identity. The reason for this extreme position is that it is a part of our presumptions on collective expression. Folk musicians and traditional musicians have their own specific way of expressing their cultures. As individuals we understand meaning from our own position and perspective, from our own individual horizons, and from our own views on these perspectives. So, what counts as important in teaching music is the role and significance of local, cultural factors and national and international perspectives and viewpoints that are important for music educators. The process of learning encompasses the social interplay between teachers and students engaged in musical learning, the 'emic' (insiders' perspective) and the 'etic' (outsiders' perspective). The latter assumes concepts (ideas and beliefs about music) and discourses (including behaviours, relationships, values, opinions, social and cultural affinities) from the teacher's own adult culture. The former (the 'emic' perspective), on the other hand, is that of the members of a culture themselves. Musical creativity practices are excellent exemplars of how diverse cultural perspectives are developed in particular contexts (Odena, 2012).

As teachers and as researchers, we live with the ambiguity inherent in curriculum mandates. Comparing curriculum content, methods, resources for delivery and assessment and how these are determined by the ministries of education in different countries highlights perspectives, strategies and practices of music education in relation to the policies and politics of the country. The context in which educational systems exist can range from a monolingual, mono-cultural society to bicultural, bilingual or multi-cultural social settings; from culturally diverse communities with a balance of traditional and contemporary musics, to teacher determined systems which give power to the individual discretion of the teacher. There are schools which are parent-community driven and schools which are centralized. All of these sites and settings call for teacher educators to network with communities regionally, nationally and internationally to offer a balance in the inclusion of music from diverse 'inside' and 'outside' musical learning cultures. Recognition of the voices of many cultural viewpoints and understanding different world views and cultural differences is facilitated by building collaborative international networks.

My own experience of multiple international collaborative projects, as exemplified and arising from research, teaching and curating arts performances, has been motivated by a common focus on creativity. I have often reflected on and empathized with accounts of scientific collaborative partnerships, as offered by John-Steiner (2000, 2002). These include a defining characteristic of collaboration as that of working together productively toward shared goals. These goals are valued at individual, communal and collective levels and achieved through jointly negotiated outcomes. Throughout, there is a dynamic interdependence of social and individual processes, particularly language in thought, that leads to the co-construction of knowledge. You need to take time to share ideas, to communicate nuanced meanings specific to particular cultures and settings and to identity and reflect on cultural differences and similarities. The development of such collaborative partnerships involves many aspects including emotional and intellectual, artistic and personal risks. Related to such risks are issues of trust, uncertainty, equity and intellectual ownership as each partner takes seriously the other's questions, skills and personal styles. Throughout the process, trust, empowerment and openness are embraced, valued and developed. Roles are adopted according to expertise, temperament, disposition and working styles, and can be negotiated and renegotiated over the life of the process. It is not easy to find time but essential that you try to have as many collaborative dialogues as needed. Recognition of the central role of dialogue, reflexivity and openness is crucial. It is a process which offers invaluable insight into 'the other' perspective but it requires empathy and open-mindedness and a willingness to offer time and an abundance of energy to engaging in lively debate with colleagues who very quickly become lifelong friends. It is truly magical.

For music teachers, the immediate future offers multiple opportunities for building new globalized and international collaborative networks, where new opportunities for creating practice and writing cultures, through international online professional exchange and conversations can happen. By looking at existing schemes (e.g. ERASMUS research schemes, social networks such as Facebook where there are blogs and wikis such as Music Creativity SRIG, professional networks such as NAME, BERA's Creativity in Education SIG and the International Society of Music Education commission dedicated to Music In Schools and Teacher Education (MISTEC)), which offer immediate membership with networks of teachers of music, teachers can engage with and develop networks and collaborative professional practices that have enduring relevance and applicability and include wider access to music across all of our diverse learning communities.

From a global learning perspective, it is likely that international collaborative ventures will play a central role in the future (John-Steiner, 2002). To this end, there is a need for teachers to: (a) acknowledge the individual and social benefits of fostering collaborative relationships; and (b) join an international network of teachers (and researchers) and engage in connecting practice with research, theory and policy.

I have learned that those individuals who contribute to collaborative partnerships do more than travel in straight, linear pathways, but rather journey along iterative pathways around which new practices are formed and framed. Collaborative partnerships involve posing new questions, being imaginative and playing with possibilities, all with a feeling of fluidity and flexibility; that is, if the process is to be a truly creative one and realized successfully within the larger structure of one's professional life.

References

Alexander, R (2000) *Culture and Pedagogy: International Comparisons in Primary Education.* Oxford: Blackwell.

Burnard, P. (2012) *Musical Creativities in Practice.* Oxford: Oxford University Press.

Jeffrey, B. (ed.) (2006) *Creative Learning practices: European experiences.* London: Tufnell Press.

John-Steiner, V. (2000, 2002) *Creative Collaboration.* New York: Oxford University Press.

McPherson and Dunbar-Hall (2001) Australia. In D.J. Hargreaves & A.C. North (eds.), *Musical Development and Learning: The international perspective.* London & New York: Continuum.

Odena, S. (Ed.) (2012) *Musical Creativity: Insights from Music Education Research.* Surrey, England: Ashgate.

Young, M. (2007) *Bringing Knowledge Back In: From Social Constructivism to Social Realism in the Sociology of Education.* London: Routledge.

Endnotes

[1] Michael Young, in his book *Bringing Knowledge Back In* draws on recent developments in the sociology of knowledge to propose answers to these key questions by reflecting on his own experience as a policy analyst and advisor in the UK, South Africa and a number of other countries. He illustrates the importance of questions about national identity (what it means to be British, to be American, to be Australian), subnational and collective identities, culture and countercultures, the emergence of the cultural politics of difference, and, at school level, the values and ideas by which teaching is informed and 'messages conveyed to children about what knowledge, what ways of thinking, talking and acting, and — through assessment — what achievements and what people are of greater and lesser worth' (Alexander, 2000: 168)

Section 4

International initiatives

Sistema: where academic, educational, musical, personal and social development all meet.

Richard J. Hallam

This chapter looks at the background to *El Sistema* and how the programme is being organized in different countries. The programme is explored through the five fundamental principles of social change, ensembles, frequency, accessibility and connectivity. By drawing on some of the many examples from around the world, it is possible to identify commonalities and differences and through that process begin to understand the phenomenon that is *El Sistema*, how it is transforming lives of young people, families and communities, and what contributes to the effectiveness of the programme in different countries. The comments and conclusions are the author's own.

El Sistema was founded in 1975 by Maestro Jose Antonio Abreu[1], a Venezuelan economist, politician and musician whose unique vision started with a small group of friends bringing more music where there was too little. Their first rehearsal in an underground garage has become something of a legend. The challenge became a concerted effort 'to find an antidote to degradation and economic deprivation through an alternative offer that could be more attractive than gangs, drug dealing, and violence' (Majno, 2012). The programme's mission statement describes its aim as 'to systematize music education and to promote the collective practice of music through symphony orchestras and choruses in order to help children and young people achieve their full potential and acquire values that favour their growth and have a positive impact on their lives in society.[2]'

As the programme grew it was organized around *núcleos*, music centres where young musicians socialize, have their lessons and rehearse in ensembles. A *núcleo* is part community centre, part second home — an always open, ever welcoming 'drop in' and 'hang out' place resonating with dozens of projects and hundreds of young people making music formally and informally. By the early 1980s there were more than 50 *núcleos* across Venezuela and the Simón Bolívar Conservatory was established with a professional faculty dedicated to intensive musical training for young musicians. Over the past 35 years Abreu has managed the growth and development of *El Sistema*, pursuing the twin goals of access and excellence on an ever-greater scale. Currently there are 285 *núcleos* in Venezuela serving more than 350,000 young people[3].

Abreu was appointed by UNESCO as a special delegate for the development and promotion of the Venezuelan youth orchestra model across the world. He was made Ambassador for Peace in 1998 and, since then, has received numerous honours and awards. Also during the late 1990s and early 2000s the Simón Bolívar Youth Orchestra embarked on increasingly ambitious European tours and the programme began to attract widespread acclaim.

Programmes across the world are expanding rapidly. Indeed, by the time this chapter is printed it will already be out of date. There are now over 50 projects in the USA with the number growing almost daily[4] while Canada has 14.[5] Over 20 projects in Europe from more than 15 countries are beginning to work more closely together and to learn from each other. There is at least one project in South Africa[6] and programmes have been started in Australia[7] and New Zealand[8]. Theodora Stathopoulos, a member of the International Society for Music Education (ISME), established a Special Interest Group in 2011 with representation from Canada, England, Germany, Greece, India, Portugal, Spain, Taiwan, and USA, which met for the first time at the ISME World conference in Greece in July 2012[9].

Some programmes are funded by governments. Others are supported through not-for-profit or philanthropic organizations and individuals. In 2008 the Ministry of Culture in São Paulo[10] launched a programme managed by Santa Marcelina Cultura and in Columbia the programme is run through the Batuta Foundation on Social Action Agreement[11]. The Dominican Republic established a non-governmental non-profit organization[12] to bring together government agencies, autonomous bodies, international institutions, companies, corporations and private individuals. In USA, the Atlanta Music Project[13] pilot was launched in 2010 at Gilbert House, an Office of Cultural Affairs cultural centre expanding in 2011 to its Coan Recreation Centre with the Zeist Foundation providing major seed funding. One of the most famous programmes in the USA is YOLA in Los Angeles[14] where Gustavo Dudamel[15], the LA Phil conductor and himself a product of the original *El Sistema* programme, is closely involved in a programme overseen by the LA Phil. South Africa has Cape Festival[16] which was launched in 2010 by Umculo/Cape Festival, an international music organization. In India[17] the programme is run by Child's Play (India) Foundation. Sistema Australia's[18] first programme, Crashendo, started in Melbourne in 2011 through a unique collaboration between Sistema Australia and various local, national, and philanthropic organizations.

In Europe, there are programmes in Austria, Bosnia, Denmark, England, Finland, France, Germany, Ireland, Italy, the Netherlands, Norway, Portugal, Romania, Scotland, Slovakia, Sweden, Switzerland and Wales. A few examples provide a flavour: the Orquestra Geracao[19] was founded in Portugal in 2007 by the National Conservatory School of Music, Amadora City Council and the Calouste Gulbenkian Foundation with support from the EQUAL (ESF) programme. 2009 saw the establishment of *El Sistema* Denmark[20] with four key partner organizations: National Organization for Disadvantaged Children and Young People, municipalities, music schools, and the Danish Amateur Orchestral Society (DAO) and, in 2011 in a socially poor area of Aarhus, Musikunik Tovshøj was founded by the Social Ministry of Denmark[21]. In Italy, the project was launched in 2010 by conductor Claudio Abbado — a longstanding musical contributor to the Venezuelan initiative — as a partnership between the national cultural organization 'Federculture' and the most established music school in the country, Scuola Musicale di Fiesole.

In Scotland, the Scottish Arts Council funded a group to visit Venezuela to observe *El Sistema*. Dr Richard Holloway, former Bishop of Edinburgh and now chair of Sistema Scotland, was a member of this group and determined to bring the movement to Scotland. He started a charity and talks were held with the Venezuelans about establishing a formal partnership. Following a performance by the Simón Bolívar Youth Orchestra of Venezuela at the Edinburgh International Festival in 2007, Maestro Abreu and Richard Holloway met and consolidated the partnership. 'Big Noise' was officially launched in 2008 with a concert in a tent with guests from the BBC Scottish Symphony Orchestra, and the National Youth Orchestra of Scotland playing alongside children from Raploch — one of the most disadvantaged areas of Stirling[22].

Most of the above programmes have started in the last five years and it is no coincidence that the programme really took off in England when the Simón Bolívar Youth Orchestra performed at the Proms in London in 2007:

> The audience was roused to a decidedly un-British frenzy. 'I am not sure anything quite like Gustavo Dudamel and his extraordinary group of young musicians has ever hit the Proms before,' wrote the music critic of the Guardian, Andrew Clements. 'There are some great youth orchestras around today, but none of them is as exciting to behold as this.' (Tunstall, 2012:121–2)

Set against a backdrop of government policy which recognized the importance of music for every child this performance turned out to be pivotal. Three million pounds of the government's funding settlement for music education for 2008–11 was allocated to setting up three pilot projects which were started in London, (led by Lambeth council); Liverpool (led by the Royal Liverpool Philharmonic Orchestra), and Norwich (led by Norwich and Norfolk Community Arts)[23]. A charity, In Harmony Sistema England, headed by Julian Lloyd Webber, was established to support the programme. The financial climate resulted in government funding being halved to £500,000 in 2011/2012 with the balance coming from a range of sources including schools, local government and philanthropists. In 2012, as part of the National Plan for Music Education, a total of £1 million each year for three years was made available to expand the programme into four more areas.

So what is this programme that is making such an enormous difference to people's lives?

El Sistema has challenged the perceived traditional wisdom. The model is not one in which instrumental technique is taught in a one to one lesson followed by a week in which the child practises alone and, when good enough, auditions to join an ensemble. What is critical is the importance of the ensemble from the beginning.

The programme ideally starts with rhythm and body expressiveness for pre-school children. Students pick up their first instruments, often recorder or percussion, aged 5. By the age of 7 they are choosing a string or wind instrument. In addition to lessons, there are sectional rehearsals and full ensemble sessions, often with the same teacher.

Regular performances are integral, thus removing much of the pressure and intensity that can sometimes be seen elsewhere. Young people rise to the occasion, even when asked to play challenging music, and a concert becomes an opportunity to share one's achievements and love of music with an audience.

Keeping the joy and fun of musical learning and music-making ever present through an immersive experience involving group learning and peer teaching is essential. The overall programme is scaled in very gradual, incremental steps so that children can continually experience success. At each level, learning takes place in the ensemble, with children constantly playing together.

One very important aspect of *El Sistema* is that it is dynamic. It is a process. Maestro Abreu says it is '*ser, no ser todavía*' (being, but not yet having become). It is constantly evolving and being adapted to meet the needs of particular children in different places. At the same time, there are clear consistencies across *núcleos*, both in assumptions and practice, and any developments follow the fundamental principles. These have been identified by Jonathan Govias, an Abreu Fellow, as social change; ensembles: the orchestra or choral experience; frequency; accessibility; connectivity[24].

It is through these five fundamentals that programmes throughout the world will now be explored.

1 Social change: the primary objective is social transformation through the pursuit of musical excellence. One happens through the other, and neither is prioritized at the expense of the other.

US writer and music educator Tricia Tunstall points out that the most significant aspect of *El Sistema* is that it is a social programme achieved through music. She quotes Dudamel as saying:

> It's about connection. In the Sistema everything is connected; the musical and the social aspects of playing music — they are never separated. Playing music together is connected with being a better citizen, with caring about other people, with working together. The orchestra, you know, it's a community. It's a little world, where you can create harmony. And of course, when you have this, connected with an artistic sensibility anything is possible. Everything is possible. (Tunstall, 2012: 24)

> We never forget that we are a social programme first. The kids work in groups because we want them to learn to work in community. (Tunstall, 2012: 34)

The majority of teachers and *núcleo* leaders are former students of the programme. They understand both the social and musical mission of the programme. They nurture both the individual person and the musician at the same time.

There is no doubt that most programmes around the world have adopted this concept. The Harmony Program in New York[25] emphasizes the influence of music-making on social development. Cape Festival in South Africa[26] refers to music as a means for social change, a way to a better future, and in the Dominican Republic[27], the project acts as a means of integrating human development, social and artistic, helping young people to make a healthy lifestyle choice and deterring them from vice and violence. Ecuador[28] states that their Symphony for Life programme is all about social inclusion, aiming to strengthen educational levels, encourage self-esteem, develop discipline, responsibility and teamwork and, through this, to reduce the risk to vulnerable groups and help them to become better students, better people and better citizens.

Orkidstra[29], administered by The Leading Note Foundation in Ottawa, and featured in the film 'Teaching the life of music',[30] is aimed at children aged five and upwards from low income neighbourhoods. Margaret Tobolowska, one of its founders, says:

> This is far more than a music program; it is a way to reach out to these children and give them a common language that breaks down barriers and grows an empathetic and caring community. (Conversation with the author, March 2012)

This is particularly relevant for *Orkidstra* which reflects Canada's diversity with nearly 30 languages spoken. But as Tina Fedeski, joint founder, says, the children share one language: music. *Orkidstra* is a music education initiative that empowers children and builds community through the universal language of music.

El Sistema's vision equally includes musical excellence, but it is not excellence as we know it. Author and arts educator Eric Booth, in Learning Matters[31], states:

> Accepted norms are completely disrupted by this work. Kids achieved faster than we normally expect or believe possible — it is establishing new norms.

How this access to excellence is achieved for the most disadvantaged young people forms the focus of the following fundamental principles.

2 Ensembles: the focus of *El Sistema* is the orchestra or choral experience.

Inspired by performances of the Simón Bolívar Orchestra, it is through the orchestra that most programmes are being developed, for example in Bahia[32], Dominican Republic[33], Ecuador[34], and New Brunswick[35]. In some cases programmes have started in collaboration with a professional orchestra such as the Auckland Philharmonia Orchestra[36], the LA Phil[37] and the Royal Liverpool Philharmonic Orchestra[38].

In Learning Matters[39], Anne Fitzgibbon, from the Harmony Program New York[40] says it is about:

> seeing the orchestra as a microcosm and teaching children all about being members of society by being members of an orchestral community. Learning to respect rules and order and organization and support one another and what people's roles are as individuals and as members of society.

Elsewhere, she speaks about the importance of:

> how early they introduce kids to the ensemble environment — it's what hooks kids, it's the fun element — it's sharing music with your peers, but it's

where children develop the social skills that are so important like listening to one another, supporting one another, collaborating with one another. (New, 2011)

Other types of ensemble feature as well as orchestras. *El Sistema has* long since had big bands and jazz, folk and chamber ensembles, choirs, prison orchestras and special ensembles for disabled young musicians. The project constantly evaluates where it is and what it needs to do. Recently Marshall Marcus, formerly Head of Music at Southbank Centre, London, was engaged to establish a Baroque Orchestra in Caracas, and to spread the performance of Baroque music by all age groups throughout the Venezuelan Sistema.

This playing together leads us to another key element of *El Sistema:* the role of peer to peer learning.

> A young girl was handed a violin for the first time and shown to a seat in the back of the violin section of her *núcleo* orchestra. The kid next to her turned and showed her where to put her hand. Like, oh, here's how you play this note. And here's how you play that note. Pedagogically, it probably wasn't perfect. But within an hour that girl felt like she was part of an orchestra. (Tunstall, 2012: 99)

Peer learning is an essential part of the overall process. *El Sistema* believes that even if you know nothing but A B C, you have the power to teach A B and C to others — and not only the power — but also the responsibility. And not only that! You yourself will learn by teaching.

Perhaps not surprisingly there was opposition to this in Venezuela when Abreu started. Most musicians of the older generation did not like what he was doing, mixing less skilled musicians with skilled ones and having them simply learn by doing together. But Abreu has never subscribed to the dichotomy of access versus excellence. He believes in both with equal zeal.

3 Frequency: *El Sistema* ensembles meet multiple times every week over extended periods.

El Sistema students live for and through their music. They play together for hours on end at *núcleos* operating after the end of the formal school day. Again, Tricia Tunstall gives us a unique insight:

> More advanced students are often frustrated that they can only come six days a week, and ask whether they can come on Sunday too. (2012: 202)

In most countries the programmes provide a daily refuge of safety, joy and fun that builds every child's self esteem and sense of worth. Attendance and behaviour are not an issue — the children want to be there for themselves, their teachers and their fellow students. Commitment and hard work are crucial to their success but a feeling of fun is never forgotten. As Tricia Tunstall states in Learning Matters[41]:

> The way behavioural issues are resolved are not reward or punishment but because the child wants to be part of something special.

In the spirit of *El Sistema*, the Harmony programme in New York requires a high degree of commitment to daily music-making by all involved. In Atlanta, children meet for two hours each day, five days per week. New Brunswick also operates for five days per week for three hours, from 1.30 to 4.30pm. In Scotland children play together on at least three days every week and daily in the school holidays. In England, the projects all have daily music-making in school, with after-school sessions on several days of the week and some music-making opportunities in the school holidays. Included in the membership criteria in England is the requirement for projects to have 'long-term, sustained and intensive involvement of the children. Commitment is developed from the children and parents and carers to ensure regular and prolonged attendance. The children are immersed in music.'[42]

4 Accessibility: *El Sistema* programmes are free, and are not selective in admission.

In order that children from the lowest income families in the most disadvantaged areas can access the power of music to transform their lives, the instruments, tuition and ensemble membership are free and open to all without audition. Several programmes in the USA, Canada, South America and Europe specifically make this point, particularly where access to instrumental lessons and ensembles has traditionally been based on the ability to pay. One of the membership criteria of In Harmony Sistema England states 'there are no financial or attainment barriers to participation. All children in the area are able to attend if they wish, but ways of reaching the particularly disadvantaged and at risk have been built in to the project.'[42] Later on, access to some of the top groups may be via an audition process and, in some cases, fees may apply for those who can afford to contribute, but inability to pay is never a deterrent. Regular involvement and commitment are important elements of most programmes as these enable the children to see rapid improvement.

But it is not only financial support that is needed for the most disadvantaged young people to benefit from these programmes. Other strategies can help to remove potential barriers to participation. Some programmes provide a healthy snack or a breakfast club before their sessions start. One English doctor wrote in an email to the project director:

> *As a local GP I was curious to investigate this activity . . . I have noticed that children have been able to talk about playing music and share this experience within the consultation. What surprised me was that these children were often those who I did not expect to chat and talk to a doctor.*
>
> *Finally but a small feature, it was heartening to see the children relishing the fruits and co-operatively clearing up. I know for many of these families access to fruits is expensive.*

These aspects can impact on funding too. In another English project, the local Primary Care Trust contributed significantly to the cost of the programme because of its positive impact on the local community.

Teachers often make home visits and quickly follow up on any absence. In Scotland, if a child wants to leave, tutors try to find out why and see if there is anything they can do differently that would change their mind. Ultimately, if the programme is just not for them, that is fine. The child can still return at any time if they change their mind[43].

5 Connectivity: every *núcleo* is linked at urban, regional and national levels, forming a cohesive network of services and opportunities for students across the country.

In exploring how *El Sistema* transfers to other countries, there are two aspects to connectivity that are considered. The first relates to the connectivity locally, regionally and nationally; the second to the connectivity with the formal music education system in schools.

In Venezuela, Sistema is a network more than a system. All the *núcleos* share an extensive core set of principles, goals and practices. There is a core repertoire of standard works across all skill levels. Local *núcleos* are part of a regional network, and each region has a director who reports to the central office of *El Sistema*.

In the USA, Sistema USA[44] is seeking to find a way of providing a network for all of the projects, many of which have started through the sheer energy and commitment of individuals. Marshall Marcus is leading the establishment of Sistema Europe but in his blog[45] cautions 'don't over-institutionalize. The best examples are often the least institutional, and the danger as *El Sistema* travels into cultures like many of ours — where process has a tendency to smother ideals — is that old chestnut: lost in translation.'

All Sistema-inspired programmes have a considerable amount of after-school provision. In some countries the programme is completely after school with no links to the school education system. In other countries there is connectivity between the out-of-school programme and the in-school music curriculum. The extent of this connectivity varies from simply knowing about the programme at one extreme to a completely integrated model, as in England, at the other. In Italy, music is not seen as an essential part of general education and Sistema Italia aims to provide additional and alternative access to music both within and alongside the school hours, with particular attention to disadvantaged families and children with special needs, operating in schools, music schools or social centres.[46] *Orkidstra*[47] in Ottawa is currently developing closer links with schools. Soundscapes[48] partnered with the Public School system to begin its first after-school year round, community-centre-based program.

In England, music education is a statutory entitlement and there is a policy for every child to learn a musical instrument. The National Plan for Music Education (2011)[49] recognizes the importance of music in the lives of young people and sets out to ensure that all have affordable access to singing, playing an instrument and making music with others, together with the opportunity to progress to the highest levels. Advocates of the *El Sistema* approach felt that for music to have the transformative impact on the personal and social lives of the most disadvantaged young people, their families and communities, something more was needed. However, it is still a requirement that there is coherence with the school programme.

Evaluation

For most programmes it is too early to learn much by way of evaluation. In 2006, as part of its due diligence before approving a loan of $150m USD, the InterAmerican Development Bank, commissioned a rigorous evaluation of the activities and impact of the programme. The report found that programme participants experienced significantly improved life and career outcomes over non-participants, including a 20% improvement in school drop-out rates[50]. The Scottish Government commissioned an independent evaluation of Big Noise which found that:

> there is evidence that Big Noise is having a positive impact on children's personal and social development, including increased confidence, self esteem, a sense of achievement and pride, improved social skills, team working skills and expanded social networks. For those children with special educational needs, behaviour issues or unsettled home lives, particular benefits include a sense of belonging, improved ability to concentrate and focus on a task, a sense of responsibility and positive behaviour change. GEN (2011: 5.27)

Independent evaluations of each of the three English pilot projects found similar outcomes and improvements[51]. For example, in Liverpool the evaluation report stated that despite less time being spent directly on numeracy and literacy, results have improved significantly. (Bowman & Burns, 2011:20–23) Ofsted, the organization that inspects and reports on schools in England, reporting on the same school, found that[52]:

> the project has brought about a cultural change in the school's wider community, with parents and families placing prime value on music education, willingly and proudly supporting their children's musical learning and attending performances.

> Parents and staff speak passionately about the way that involvement in music has changed children's attitudes and expectations. As one parent said, 'music has given our children respect for themselves, respect for each other, and respect for education'.

Concluding thoughts

How each country adopts and adapts the programme to fit most effectively into its own culture and society is a decision that each must make, including how the programme is administered and funded. The concept of the programme is challenging, especially where funding is driven by targets and clear measurable outcomes, where practitioners and policy makers are looking for documents and programmes of study that define what is taught and how. But it is a problem that must be solved, at least in part, if the phenomenon that is *El Sistema* is to transfer successfully to other countries around the world. For therein also lies a danger: the worldwide potential of the programme to change lives for the better could be at risk. Insufficient funding, or misunderstood values and ethos, will result in diluted versions of *El Sistema* that will fail to have the enormous impact associated with the programme.

It is interesting that in Venezuela, Abreu always kept the programme away from the government's culture and education departments. It was previously housed by different social service departments. Responsibility then moved to the office of the Vice President and, in 2011, oversight moved to the office of the President. For such an important programme, that cuts across the remits of social, health, education, culture and justice, this is an important consideration.

The final words should go to the founder, Maestro Abreu:

> Our success, and the fact that the government supported us, allowed me to show the remainder of the country that an orchestra could be an instrument for social change. (Tunstall, 2012: 72)
>
> There is no better way to build the life of a community than children playing music together. (Tunstall, 2012: 153).

References

Books and online publications:

Burns, S. & Bewick, P. (2011) In Harmony Liverpool, Interim Report: Year Two. In Harmony/ DfE/ Liverpool Philharmonic. http://ihse.org.uk/evaluation-liverpool-2011 (accessed 18/09/12).

GEN (2011) Evaluation of Big Noise, Sistema Scotland. Edinburgh, Scottish Government.

Majno, M. (2012) From the model of *El Sistema* in Venezuela to current applications: learning and integration through collective music education. Annals of the New York Academy of Sciences, Vol. 1252, 56–64. New York: NYAS www.nyas.org/Publications/Archive.aspx (accessed 18/09/12).

Tunstall, T. (2012) *Changing Lives: Gustavo Dudamel, El Sistema and the Transformative Power of Music.* New York: W.W. Norton & Company.

Film:

New, D. (dir.) (2011). *Teaching the Life of Music.* Toronto: Filmblanc.

Further reading

Corona Youth Music Project in Queens, New York. www.nucleocorona.org/ (accessed 28/04/2012)

Toronto. www.sistema-toronto.ca (accessed 4/6/2012)

Kalikolehua Hawaii. http://kalikolehua.com/ (accessed 28/04/2012)

Superar Central Europe. http://superar.eu/ (accessed 1/5/2012

Germany: an instrument for every child. www.jedemkind.de/ (accessed 1/5/2012)

France www.orchestres-en-choeur.fr/. (accessed 1/5/2012)

Buskaid South Africa. www.buskaid.org.za/ (accessed 1/5/2012)

Endnotes

1. http://en.wikipedia.org/wiki/Jos%C3%A9_Antonio_Abreu (accessed 2/7/2012)
2. www.fesnojiv.gob.ve/en/mission-and-vision.html (accessed on 18/2/2012)
3. www.fesnojiv.gob.ve/ (accessed 8/5/2012)
4. http://elsistemausa.org/ (accessed 28/4/2012)
5. http://jonathangovias.com/2012/02/16/el-sistema-in-canada-2012-update/ (accessed 28/4/2012)
6. www.capefestival.com/ (accessed 1/5/2012)
7. www.sistemaaustralia.com.au/programs.html (accessed 28/4/2012)
8. www.apo.co.nz/sistema-aotearoa/ (accessed 5/5/2012)
9. www.isme.org/index.php?option=com_content&view=article&id=129:special-interest-groups-sigs&catid=43:isme-2012&Itemid=26#sig3 (accessed 26/4/2012)
10. www.gurisantamarcelina.org.br (accessed 29/4/2012)
11. www.fundacionbatuta.org/ (accessed 1/5/2012)
12. www.fosjrd.com/ (accessed 1/5/2012)
13. atlantamusicproject.org/ (accessed 28/04/2012)
14. www.laphil.com/education/yola.cf (accessed 5/5/2012)
15. www.gustavodudamel.com/content/biography (accessed 28/5/2012)
16. www.capefestival.com/ (accessed 1/5/2012)
17. www.childsplayindia.org/ (accessed 1/5/2012)
18. http://sistemaaustralia.com.au/ (accessed 28/04/2012)
19. www.orquestra.geracao.aml.pt/o-projecto (accessed 2/5/2012)
20. www.elsistema.dk/ (accessed 29/04/2012)
21. www.aarhusmusikskole.dk/da/Projektor.aspx (accessed 30/4/2012)
22. www.makeabignoise.org.uk/ *(accessed 5/5/2012)*
23. www.ihse.org.uk (accessed 5/5/2012)
24. http://jonathangovias.com/author/
25. http://harmonyprogram.cuny.edu/about-the-program (accessed 28/4/2012)
26. www.capefestival.com/el_sistema.php (accessed 1/5/2012)
27. www.fosjrd.com/site/sobre_nosotros.html (accessed 1/5/2012)
28. www.sinfoniaporlavida.com/ (accessed 1/5/2012)
29. www.orkidstra.ca (accessed 28/4/2012)
30. www.filmblanc.com/ *(accessed 5/5/2012)*
31. http://vimeo.com/40731308 (accessed 28/04/2012)
32. www.neojiba.org/ (accessed 1/5/2012)
33. www.fosjrd.com/ (accessed 1/5/2012)
34. www.sinfoniaporlavida.com/ (accessed 1/5/2012)
35. www.nbyo-ojnb.com/ (accessed 5/5/2012)
36. http://apo.co.nz/ (accessed 5/5/2012)

37 http://losangeles.broadwayworld.com/printcolumn.php?id=372047 (accessed 1/5/2012)
38 www.ihse.org.uk
39 http://vimeo.com/40734996 (accessed 28/4/2012)
40 http://harmonyprogram.cuny.edu/about-the-program (accessed 28/4/2012)
41 http://vimeo.com/40734996 (accessed 28/4/2012)
42 http://ihse.org.uk/membership (accessed 19/09/2012)
43 http://makeabignoise.org.uk/sistema-scotland/ (accessed 7/5/2012)
44 http://elsistemausa.org/ (accessed 28/4/2012)
45 http://marshallmarcus.wordpress.com/ (accessed2/5/2012)
46 http://federculture.it/ (accessed 1/5/2012)
47 www.orkidstra.ca (accessed 27/4/2012)
48 www.soundscapeshr.org/ (accessed 28/4/2012)
49 www.education.gov.uk/schools/teachingandlearning/curriculum/a00200352/national-plan-for-music-education (accessed 2/7/2012)
50 http://elsistema.files.wordpress.com/2012/03/iadb-evaluation.pdf
51 http://ihse.org.uk/research (accessed 11/5/2012)
52 www.ofsted.gov.uk/inspection-reports/find-inspection-report/provider/ELS/134723 Ofsted July 2010 www.ofsted.gov.uk/provider/files/967917/urn/134723.pdf and February 2011 www.ofsted.gov.uk/provider/files/1512829/urn/134723.pdf

Achieving through Diversity: music competitions and their role in music education across Europe

Claire Goddard

The British can boast a well-established and highly-regarded instrumental examination system, a diverse spectrum of regional competitions and festivals, and the BBC Young Musicians television competition. Nevertheless, music competitions have not and do not at present play a particularly significant role in music education in the United Kingdom. In mainland Europe it is a different story. In many countries music competitions for young people are well-known national structures and play a key role in the music education system, providing assessment and comparison possibilities and valuable opportunities for young people to make music together. Young musicians have the opportunity to progress to higher levels within competitions and even perform on an international level, enriching their musical learning with new insights and experiences.

This chapter will look first of all at practices in some of the countries and regions of Europe, giving examples of competitions and how they function in relation to the particular circumstances of that country. This will be followed by an examination of the challenge of diversity facing the different competitions and music education systems as they seek the best ways of integrating disciplines such as jazz, pop, rock, folk or world music into existing curriculums and assessment procedures. Finally, the role of the European Union of Music Competitions for Youth (EMCY) will be explored, looking at its pan-European function in the complex and constantly developing tapestry of music education and assessment.

Some music competition structures in Europe

The largest national youth music competition in Europe, and one which has served as a point of reference for many others, is the German *Jugend musiziert* (literally 'youth makes music'). Established in 1963 and winner in 2011 of a special ECHO Klassik Award (the German equivalent of the Classical BRIT Awards), *Jugend musiziert* holds a central position in German music education. It is a household name and has inspired a range of similar initiatives within the wider education sector. Every autumn around 24,000 young people, mostly between the ages of eight and 20, register for the regional competitions that start the yearly *Jugend musiziert* cycle. The competition is for citizens and residents of Germany and also pupils of German international schools abroad who have their own regional competitions.

The top prize winners at the regional level (except in the lowest age category for children under the age of nine) win the chance to participate in the state competitions in early spring. The first prize winners of the state competitions (except again for the lowest age category, at state level for children up to the age of eleven) qualify for the national final which is held in late May or early June in a different city each year. For a week that city comes alive with music: alongside the evaluated performances there are a variety of concerts and workshops and the streets are filled with many highly talented young buskers keen to top up their pocket money. In 2012, 2,068 young people participated in the national final (some of them in more than one category) and 1,251 first, second and third prizes were awarded to soloists, ensembles and young accompanists. 337 of these were first prizes. The prizes consist of specially commissioned art works and the nature and number of the prizes reveals much about the philosophy of the competition: it is not about awarding money prizes to the very top musicians, rather about rewarding achievement on a much wider level and providing a stimulus for high quality music education.

The competition is open to players of a very wide range of instruments, with a particular focus on chamber music. A three-year cycle means that everyone can participate every year, either as a soloist or in an ensemble. The cycle of categories (table 1) demonstrates this:

	2013	2014	2015
Solo categories (with/without accompaniment)	<ul><li>(bowed) string instruments</li><li>accordion</li><li>percussion</li><li>*mallets* (tuned percussion keyboard instruments)</li><li>pop singing</li></ul>	<ul><li>piano</li><li>harp</li><li>voice</li><li>drum kit (pop)</li><li>guitar (pop)</li></ul>	<ul><li>wind instruments</li><li>plucked string instruments</li><li>bass (pop)</li><li>musical</li><li>organ</li></ul>
Ensemble categories	<ul><li>piano and wind instrument (except recorder*) duo</li><li>piano chamber music</li><li>vocal ensemble</li><li>plucked string ensembles</li><li>harp ensembles</li><li>*Alte Musik* (early music)</li></ul> *Recorders must be accompanied by cembalo and are therefore included in the early music category.*	<ul><li>wind ensemble</li><li>string ensemble</li><li>accordion ensemble</li><li>contemporary music</li></ul>	<ul><li>piano and string instrument duo</li><li>*Kunstlied* duo (voice and piano)</li><li>percussion ensemble</li><li>piano (four hands)</li><li>'special ensembles' (an open category for the ensemble performance of works of the classical, romantic, late romantic, and classical modern periods)</li></ul>

Table 1: Cycle of categories for *Jugend musiziert*, based on the 2012 *Ausschreibung* (see references)

This cycle provides young musicians and their teachers with constantly evolving challenges. It encourages them to form chamber music ensembles, explore new repertoire and meet new friends. Even the solo categories support this philosophy as soloists are encouraged to work with young accompanists who are also assessed and win prizes. New categories are often added at state level and, if proved successful, are introduced later in other states and at the national finals.

An integral part of the *Jugend musizert* programme has long been a residential chamber music course in the summer holidays for national prize winners. Here, like-minded young people have the chance to tackle new musical challenges together and explore new repertoire under the guidance of renowned musicians. A recent addition to the programme for national prize winners is WESPE (Weekends of Special Prizes). A variety of sponsors offer large money prizes but these competitions are primarily designed to test and inspire the young musicians in a new way: categories include the performance of their own compositions; of works by female composers; of an entire sonata; of contemporary works, and even of works by composers ostracized during the National Socialist regime. The competitions take place around the summer break from school with the intention that the young musicians tackle these challenges with less support from teachers than for the main competition.

Jugend musiziert may be a competition but participants are not competing against each other: the musicians are assessed against a nationally, and indeed internationally, recognized 25-point system and there is no upper or lower limit on the number of prizes. The same evaluation method is used by the expert juries for all age categories, disciplines, and levels, and the value of gaining prizes at the different levels of this competition is widely recognized outside of the music education sector, for instance in university selection criteria for non-musical courses. Each round of the competition provides goals for pupils and teachers to work towards and is followed up by evaluation meetings with a juror. These are always held before the results are announced as experience has shown this to be more effective because at this point the participants are more receptive. The meetings are specifically for the young participants but teachers and parents are also welcome to attend and can also benefit from the advice given.

There are of course many points of comparison between *Jugend musiziert* and the British music examination system. Whilst the breadth offered by aural training, scales and sight-reading is missing (and the British are internationally renowned for their sight-reading skills), the chamber music opportunities provided by *Jugend musiziert* are greater. *Jugend musiziert* provides German pupils with a different type of musical challenge each year. Together with their teachers they put together a concert performance and have the opportunity to refine this and learn from their experiences as they progress to higher levels of the competition. Evaluation is by expert juries consisting of at least three members on a regional level, more on the state and national levels, most of whom must be specialists in the instrument in question. The one-off evaluation in written form offered by the British examination system, often by a non-specialist, if expert, examiner in a small room examination setting is a different experience. These examinations are of course complemented by the large range of regional competitions across the country but the level of these varies considerably and there are few connections between them or possibilities to progress as a matter of course to higher levels.

The complex structure and wide scope of *Jugend musiziert* is reliant on a dense network of musical institutions across the country and a high level of public funding at regional, state and national levels. Whilst the regional and state competitions are preliminary rounds to the national final, they are also significant events in their own right, with many extra concerts and activities organized for prize winners at these levels, whether or not they go on to win further prizes. Education in Germany is largely governed at state level (there is for instance no centralized *Abitur* examination (equivalent to GCE A levels) for the whole country) and this is reflected in the music education provision. The national *Jugend musiziert* structure benefits from strong state networks and institutions, and serves an additional purpose in making connections between them and enabling nationwide comparison for participants, teachers, and all involved in music education.

Jugend musiziert is not the only national youth music competition which sees its main function as providing the backbone for a rounded and high quality music education in its home country. The model has served as an example for many Western European countries and in particular for Austria and Switzerland. The structure and content of the competition is of course adapted to the particular needs and circumstances of the country in question and it is important to note that the Swiss competition receives no public funding. The French and Spanish national competitions do not have the comprehensive structure or outreach of the Germanic countries but national competitions are key activities for the national music networks: *Juventudes Musicales de España* and the *Confédération Musicale de France*. The Spanish *Concurso Permanente de Jóvenes Intérpretes* takes place for specified categories twice a year and is hosted each time by a different regional section of the national network. In 2012 it is taking place for the 77th and 78th time. The national structure also provides the prize winners with a wide range of concert opportunities organized by the regional and national associations.

Some smaller countries have expanded their national competitions to an international level. At the *Concours Luxembourgeois pour Jeunes Solistes,* for instance, the national competition is opened every year in certain categories to allow wider European participation and offer further scope and possibilities for comparison. All jurors at this competition come from outside Luxembourg: this is to avoid possible conflicts of interest which are more likely in such a small country, but also adds an interesting and beneficial international dimension to the event.

Many national competitions incorporate European concerts into their programme featuring prize winners from competitions in other countries. The concerts provide a wider context and opportunity for comparison whilst being a beneficial and exciting experience for the young musicians involved. Every year, the national *Jugend musiziert* competition includes a concert presenting the outcomes of the previous year's residential chamber music course together with performances from two prize winners from other national EMCY member competitions. In 2012 these were from the Netherlands and Switzerland. Another example is the annual European concert at the Norwegian national competition *Ungdommens Musikkmesterskap* where the prizes are announced alongside performances from two prize winners from other national youth music competitions as well as the 'Musician of the Year' from the previous Norwegian competition.

In Russia and Eastern Europe, the music education systems are generally focused more towards solo performers and ensuring high levels of achievement. Competitions therefore have a special status and international competitions for younger children are more common. In these countries the role of the teacher is particularly prominent and they are rewarded for their pupils' success, for instance with special prizes for teachers at competitions and/or subsequent recognition and promotion at the music education institution at which they teach. Achieving competition success for their pupils is often seen as a measure of a teacher's capabilities and thus competitions take on an extra significance in the assessment and appraisal of music teaching itself.

In contrast to professional music competitions for older musicians such as the Leeds International Piano Competition, which are more concerned with launching careers, international youth music competitions in Europe see themselves as an important part of the education process, working to identify extraordinarily talented young musicians and provide them with the necessary promotion and support to enable them to fulfil their potential. A particularly good example is the British-based Menuhin Competition for violinists under the age of 22 which is held every two years in a different location (in 2012, for the first time outside Europe, in Beijing). Yehudi Menuhin founded this competition in 1983 with the intention of bringing together exceptionally talented young violinists from across the globe in an enriching, stimulating and friendly environment where the focus is on education and cultural exchange rather than winning prizes. Participants are encouraged to stay for the whole competition period and those who do not reach the finals receive the opportunity to give extra performances as well as passing on their expertise (and learning a great deal about themselves and the skills involved in teaching in the process) to local schools by holding their own master classes. The outreach activities offered by the competition bring the young musicians from across the globe into contact with school children and the community in and around the host city.

The challenge of diversity

While international competitions are mostly intended for players of a specific instrument and relatively independent in status, national youth music competitions have a duty to serve the music educational needs of their own country and to offer assessment and comparison possibilities for the disciplines being taught in (music) schools. Until very recently music education and competitions have been predominantly based on the classical canon but they are now facing the challenge of providing for 'non-classical' categories such as jazz, rock, pop, folk and world music. The term 'non-classical' is indeed itself problematic in its vagueness and connotations but has entered use due to the wide range of artistic styles in question. Educational competitions in certain disciplines such as rock or pop are a new phenomenon and are developing partly as a reaction to high profile commercial television contests which can have a very negative impact on the young people involved. However, specialist competitions in other disciplines such as jazz and folk have existed for some time and have developed their own traditions and standards.

As presented in the table of categories offered in the three-year *Jugend musiziert* cycle, voice, drum kit, guitar and bass are all currently offered as 'pop' solo categories at all levels of the competition. This is a recent development and one that remains controversial. At the moment, group assessment for pop music is only available at state level in Berlin. Further categories currently offered only at state level include bağlama (a Turkish plucked string instrument) ensemble in Berlin, reflecting the large Turkish population in this city, and dulcimer in Bavaria (linked to the folk tradition in the Alpine region). These two categories exemplify the manifold challenges of promoting and protecting cultural diversity through music education[1]: on the one hand it is important to encourage young people to engage with the traditional music and cultural heritage of their region and on the other it is crucial to adapt to the needs of our increasingly multicultural societies and to aid integration and social cohesion.

By contrast, in the Austrian and Swiss national competitions the dulcimer is included in the main competition programme but separate competitions have been developed for jazz, rock and pop which are for groups rather than soloists. The fact that these are organized by an established national youth music institution affords them a certain status. However, it is believed that the particular requirements of these musical disciplines need a specialist approach. Venues are chosen to suit these musical styles and to ensure that the appropriate equipment is available. It has been claimed that the repertoire for these competitions is even more demanding than for the classical competitions given the requirement that the musicians include their own compositions in their competition programme, but this is hotly debated.

As we have seen, Germany's *Jugend musiziert* intentionally integrates its pop categories into the main competition. It is believed that this puts both classical and pop on the same level, creating new audiences for both and raising the status of pop music education. Opponents of this strategy argue that it is based upon the assumption that non-classical musical styles must be assimilated with classical music in order to be acknowledged and afforded a certain status. For them, it should be more a case of establishing parity between the different styles. Moreover, the organizers of classical music competitions have specific types of expertise and may not be best equipped to provide optimal conditions for non-classical disciplines.

In the field of jazz, both of these approaches have been implemented successfully. In the Netherlands, a separate competition is held under the umbrella of the *Prinses Christina Concours*, while in Belgium jazz is integrated into the diverse tapestry of disciplines covered by the *Belfius Classics* competition. The latter is very open, offering categories in all disciplines taught in at least two Belgian 'academies' and organizing them under the general headings of: *musique, création musicale, arts de la parole and création littéraire'*. It is interesting to note that the German Music Council, which organizes *Jugend musiziert*, also holds a completely separate annual jazz competition called *Jugend jazzt* which was founded in 1997. This is for ensembles and big bands with the winners of the state competitions participating in the *Bundesbegegnung* (literally 'national meeting point'). This national event is different from the *Bundeswettbewerb* ('national competition') of *Jugend musiziert* as the emphasis is not on the competition aspect (although significant money prizes as well as recording, concert and mentoring prizes are on offer), but rather on the event as a whole which is designed to help the young musicians take their first steps towards a successful career.

It is hoped that this outline has made it clear that there is a broad range of successful strategies and philosophies regarding the categories offered for assessment at national competitions and it would be both inaccurate and dangerous to claim that there is only one perfect approach. Indeed, competition organizers and the music education sector as a whole are exploring these new possibilities together and asking similar questions: What assessment criteria can we use for these 'new' categories? What repertoire and skills should be prescribed? What new logistical requirements arise and how do we deal with these? Can existing models be adapted or must new ones be developed? Where are the points of contact and comparison between different artistic disciplines? How can we assure quality and avoid dumbing down? Will offering a wider range of musical options lead to even fewer (or maybe more) young people being interested in classical music? What are the consequences for the future?

EMCY and its role

The European Union of Music Competitions for Youth (EMCY) cannot provide answers to these questions but has an important role to play as a platform for the exchange of experience and ideas. It was founded in 1970 and continues to grow at a steady pace, currently counting 16 national and 27 international competitions in its membership, with representation from 22 European countries spanning the continent from Portugal to Russia. It is one of a range of specialist European networks active in the field of music education which work closely together in the development and implementation of policy and practice. These organizations operate at the tips of the many interlocking pyramids that make up the European music education tapestry and indeed the music and arts sector as a whole. EMCY's General Assemblies, conferences for national or international competitions, and seminars on specific topics such as non-classical categories bring together representatives of youth music competitions to share, learn, debate, inspire and be inspired by the activities of others.

It is EMCY's guiding principle that competitions are a learning experience: winning a prize should not be the end, but rather the beginning of the next stage of this educational process. EMCY membership provides an extra level in that prize winners are offered online profiles on the EMCY website, information about international competitions that would be of interest to them and, most importantly, invitations to give concerts and take part in master classes outside their home country. Performance experience is of course vital for young gifted musicians, even more so in a foreign country and together with other young Europeans. EMCY was founded upon co-operation between national music competitions which offered European concerts for each other's prize winners: such exchanges remain at the heart of EMCY's activities more than 40 years later.

EMCY membership is a quality label for a competition and members must abide by EMCY's Quality Standards for Youth Music Competitions 'in the interest of fairness, the educational process and competition best practice'[2]. It cannot be denied that in some instances competition practice can be dubious, that juries do not fulfil their task fairly due to conflicts of interest, and that participation can be a negative experience for both pupils and teachers. EMCY therefore has an important responsibility to be an advocate for fairness, to foster the educational value of youth music competitions, and to ensure that the competitions that display the EMCY logo actively propagate these standards. Young musicians, their teachers, their parents, and the music sector as a whole must be able to trust in the results and the educational benefit of these competitions.

The EMCY Quality Standards cover many aspects of competition organization including repertoire, length of programme, prizes, number of prize winners, rehearsal times, oral and printed information and, most importantly, jury work. It is not, however, EMCY's purpose to closely regulate or control its members, nor to make them all the same. On the contrary, EMCY respects and treasures the variety of traditions in music competition practice across Europe and the close links with the music educational structures of a particular region. The Quality Standards are recommendations and need not be completely adhered to as long as it is clear that the competition is operating fairly. The guidelines have been particularly welcomed by those new to competition practice and organization, and new competitions are at present being established, based on these internationally recognized standards. Of course, EMCY cannot guarantee a positive competition experience for all, nor can it wipe out all badly organized or unfair competitions across Europe. However, by raising the profile of EMCY membership and what it signifies, competitions which do not operate fairly will start to struggle to attract participants and (financial) support. It is a long process but one of vital importance to the music education sector across the continent and beyond.

The Quality Standards also have a particular value in the current non-classical categories debate. It is clear that quality is a key factor in music education provision[3] and is particularly crucial for assessment procedures and therefore competitions. The Quality Standards were created with classical music competitions in mind but also with the intention of keeping possibilities open for other categories. EMCY is thus described in this document as 'an organization of music competitions for voice or instruments/ genres which have a coherent system of education'. This definition is now at the heart of a debate within the EMCY network and a starting point for further investigation into the compatibility of these guidelines with non-classical categories. In the long term, it may be the case that these guidelines must be adapted or separate guidelines for different disciplines produced. It may even be the case that EMCY chooses to return to its roots as an organization for classical music. Whatever happens, the issue of quality must remain at the heart of the debate.

Learning together across frontiers

In conclusion, just as European countries have a wide range of music education systems, so they are home to a diverse spectrum of youth music competitions which are closely linked to regional educational structures, traditions and practices. The United Kingdom may have a music education system that is distinctive from its European neighbours but it is certainly not the case that all of the other 26 member states of the European Union are sharing an identical approach. 'United in Diversity' is indeed a very fitting motto for the European Union and for the music education and competitions within it.

Indeed, the function of youth music competitions in any country is very closely linked to the perception of competition in that society in general. For instance, in Germany, competitions are seen as an effective method of creating interest and wide participation in a field of activity or initiative. Further east, in Poland or Russia, exceptional talent is more prized and seen as a reflection of a successful society. The implementation and role of competitions in music education thus varies considerably from country to country but an important common educational purpose prevails nonetheless. It is upon such foundations that European co-operation can develop and thrive: differences cannot be ignored but must play second fiddle to finding common ground and mutually advantageous methods of co-operation.

Music educators across Europe actively advocate a more joined-up and multifaceted approach to music education. Music competitions can be an effective strategy to achieve this, for instance through national structures such as *Jugend musiziert* or through the incorporation of 'non-classical' categories. Moreover, few would argue against the need for a quality system of assessment with wide recognition across the sector. A stronger network of quality youth music competitions across the United Kingdom would certainly not be detrimental to the education system as a whole but there are few who would identify this as a particular priority or necessity. British music educators can nevertheless learn a great deal from the music education practices of our European neighbours and adopt or adapt those that are most relevant to their daily practice. Equally, colleagues on the continent could profit a great deal from a better understanding of the successes and difficulties of the British system. Working across boundaries to create a more joined-up music education sector is a hot topic at the moment in the United Kingdom: why not work across national boundaries and let our European colleagues contribute to helping us along the path?

Further reading:

An overview in English of the national and international member competitions of EMCY can be found at www.emcy.org/member-competitions as well as links to the websites of the individual competitions. National competitions mostly only publish information in their own language whereas international competitions are required to have the relevant information also in English.

Some information (in German) about *Jugend musiziert* can be found at www.jugend-musiziert.org, where the yearly *Ausschreibung* (competition rules booklet) is available as a PDF for download.

Information (in English) about the Echo Klassik Award can be found at www.echoklassik.de/en/klassik-startseite/.

EMCY's Quality Standards for Youth Music Competitions can be downloaded at www.emcy.org/about-emcy/quality-standards.

More information about the 2005 UNESCO Convention on the Protection and Promotion of the Diversity of Cultural Expressions and related actions can be found at www.unesco.org/new/en/culture/themes/cultural-diversity/2005-convention.

The UNESCO Seoul Agenda and related documents can be downloaded at www.unesco.org/new/en/culture/themes/creativity/arts-education.

The European Music Council's Bonn Declaration is available at www.emc-imc.org/fileadmin/user_upload/Cultural_Policy/Bonn_Declaration.pdf.

Endnotes

[1] Almost all European countries as well as the European Union are parties to the 2005 UNESCO *Convention on the Protection and Promotion of the Diversity of Cultural Expressions* and are legally obliged to implement this and report on their actions.

[2] The Quality Standards can be read and downloaded at www.emcy.org/about-emcy/quality-standards.

[3] Quality is one of the three goals identified by the UNESCO *Seoul Agenda, Goals for the Development of Arts Education*: 'GOAL 2: Assure that arts education activities and programmes are of a high quality in conception and delivery'. This is reflected in the European Music Council's Bonn Declaration which relates the Seoul Agenda to music education in Europe.

From Seoul to Bonn: a journey through international and European music education policies

Simone Dudt

This chapter will look at international and European cultural policy contexts for music education. It will explore strategies developed by the United Nations Educational, Scientific and Cultural Oraganization (UNESCO) with regard to arts education and give a brief overview on the policies in place at European Union (EU) level. Finally, it will introduce the policies of the European Music Council in the field of music education and give an example of how international policy documents for music education have been used for advocacy work.

UNESCO and arts education

The UNESCO web portal on arts education gives a comprehensive justification for UNESCO's engagement with arts education:

> Facing the [. . .] fundamental requirements of the 21st century, it has also become crucial to adopt our awareness and knowledge with shifting conditions of socio-cultural changes, particularly in acknowledging the diversity of cultures in today's multicultural societies. In this regard, education and learning are asked to play a fundamental role in nurturing a creative environment.[1]

Arts education was addressed by UNESCO as early as its third General Conference in 1948, though only in respect of it having a place in education as a whole (UNESCO, 1948, para 2.54).

In 1996 UNESCO published the report 'Learning: the treasure within' (Delors et al. 1996) which was produced by the International Commission on Education for the 21st Century under the direction of Jacques Delors. The report stresses the importance of education through art and creativity. Its basic assumption is that education throughout life is based upon four pillars: learning to know, learning to do, learning to live together and learning to be. In the introduction to the report Delors states:

> There is [. . .] every reason to place renewed emphasis on the moral and cultural dimensions of education, enabling each person to grasp the individuality of other people and to understand the world's erratic

progression towards a certain unity; but this process must begin with self-understanding through an inner voyage whose milestones are knowledge, meditation and the practice of self-criticism. (Delors et al., 1996: 17)

The 30th session of the UNESCO's General Conference in November 1999 adopted an appeal by the Director-General of UNESCO for the promotion of arts education and creativity at school as part of the construction of a culture of peace. The appeal includes the following statement:

The school of the 21st century must be able to anticipate new needs by according a special place to the teaching of artistic values and subjects in order to encourage creativity, which is a distinctive attribute of the human species. Creativity is our hope. (UNESCO, 1999: 69)

This appeal marked the beginning of UNESCO's growing interest in arts education and initiated its official position in 'promoting the cross-disciplinary role of arts teaching as a fundamental element in education, especially in strengthening the promotion of cultural diversity'. It describes the arts as 'integral to life: function creation and learning are intertwined' and refers to learning through the arts as well as learning in the arts.[2]

The *Convention on the Protection and Promotion of the Diversity of Cultural Expressions* (UNESCO, 2005) is widely considered as the 'Magna Carta' of international cultural policy, since it defines a human's right to cultural self-determination by international law. The central issue is the acknowledgement of the right of all nations to an independent cultural policy. Article 10 of the Convention calls for educational and public awareness programmes for cultural diversity, co-operation with diverse partners and educational, training and exchange programmes in the field of cultural industries. The Convention has been ratified by 123 UNESCO member states as well as the European Union (as of 18 July 2012), and the first reports on the progress of its implementation were collected by UNESCO in 2012.

The UNESCO road map for arts education

The first World Conference on Arts Education was held in Lisbon in March 2006. All UN regions had been working to prepare this conference since 2003 with meetings taking place in Australia, Korea, Lithuania, Columbia, Trinidad and Tobago. The outcome of the conference was the *Road Map for Arts Education* (UNESCO, 2006), a 20-page document that provides a practical and theoretical framework with guidance for strengthening arts education worldwide. The challenge of a document such as the Road Map is the need to embrace a broad variety of cultures while at the same time establishing a common notion of 'art'. This is reflected in the chapter on 'arts fields' where an inclusive approach towards the definition of arts is chosen: 'any listings of arts fields must be seen as pragmatic categorization [. . .]. A tentative list might include performing arts (dance, drama, music, etc.), literature and poetry, craft, design, digital arts, storytelling, heritage, visual arts and film, media, and photography.' (UNESCO 2006: 7).

The Road Map concludes with recommendations directed towards all those involved in arts education:

- Educators, parents, artists and directors of schools and educational institutions
- Government ministries and policy makers
- UNESCO and other intergovernmental and non-governmental organizations

Taking into consideration that all these stakeholders are relevant for the successful delivery of arts education on a local, national or regional level, the Road Map demonstrates a broad approach towards cultural policy where all involved are obligated to become actively engaged. Therefore, partnerships and co-operation form a central part of the recommendations.

The Seoul agenda: goals for the development of arts education

The second UNESCO World Conference on Arts Education was hosted by the Korean Government in May 2010. The outcome of the conference was the Seoul Agenda (UNESCO, 2010), an action plan that was developed collaboratively by the International Advisory Committee (IAC) and the participants of the Seoul conference. It is a tool to renew the commitment to arts education and a resource for advocacy (cf. O'Farrell, 2010: 12). The Seoul Agenda is a continuation of the implementation of the Road Map and 'integrates the substance of the Road Map within a structure of three broad goals' (UNESCO 2010: 2).

- Goal 1: Ensure that arts education is accessible as a fundamental and sustainable component of a high quality renewal of education
- Goal 2: Assure that arts education activities and programmes are of a high quality in conception and delivery
- Goal 3: Apply arts education principles and practices to contribute to resolving the social and cultural challenges facing today's world

Each of the goals includes strategies and action items.

In October 2010 the Executive Board of UNESCO recommended the acceptance of the Seoul Agenda by the member states and introduced the idea of an international arts education week, which was celebrated for the first time from 21–27 May 2012.

The above outline shows how UNESCO has continuously developed its approach to arts education from a perspective that is solely focused on general education to a broader concept that also acknowledges the diversity of learners and learning environments where arts education take place.

Arts education and the European Union

The process of European co-operation was started in order to facilitate economy and trade after World War II and to build a union of peace amongst the European countries through economic co-operation. The Maastricht Treaty (1992) is the founding document of the European Union in its present form and it includes policy areas such as culture and education. The article of the treaty relating to culture allows the EU 'to take action in the field of culture in order to safeguard, disseminate and develop culture in Europe'[3]. Education and training are seen as key factors to transform the EU into 'a world-leading knowledge-based society and economy'[4].

At EU level, the policy areas of culture and education are subject to the principle of subsidiarity because this competence lies at member state level and the EU may only intervene if it is able to act more effectively than individual member states. Actions which the EU can take include promoting co-operation between different EU countries and complementing existing activities while at the same time respecting national and regional diversity. The EU installed a culture programme that supports cultural co-operation projects, whilst through its Lifelong Learning Programme (LLP), education and training opportunities in the fields of schools (Comenius), higher education (Erasmus), vocational education and training (Leonardo da Vinci) and adult education (Grundtvig) are supported.

Under the new strategic framework for European co-operation in education and training (European Union, 2009; known as ET 2020) one of the four objectives is 'enhancing creativity and innovation, including entrepreneurship, at all levels of education and training' including the promotion of cultural awareness. Currently, all EU programmes are under negotiation for the new budget cycle that will start in 2014.

European agenda for culture in a globalizing world

In November 2007, the European ministers of culture (Culture Council) agreed on a 'European Agenda for Culture' (European Commission, 2007). Importantly, the agenda not only refers to the 2005 UNESCO Convention on the Diversity of Cultural Expressions but re-confirms the EU's commitment as a signatory party to the Convention.

The introduction of the European Agenda for Culture states:

> Culture lies at the heart of human development and civilization. Culture is what makes people hope and dream [. . .]. Respect for cultural and linguistic diversity and promotion of a common cultural heritage lies at the very heart of the European project. (European Commission 2007: 2)

The European Agenda for Culture reflects a growing recognition within the EU that culture has a unique and indispensable role to play. The objectives of the agenda are:

- the promotion of cultural diversity and intercultural dialogue
- the promotion of culture as a catalyst for creativity in the framework of the Lisbon Strategy for growth, employment, innovation and competitiveness[5]
- the promotion of culture as a vital element in the Union's international relations

These objectives will be met by establishing new partnerships and forms of communication. As a result, a structured dialogue between the political field (the EU and its member states) and civil society was started.

The dialogue partners representing civil society came together in the three so-called culture sector platforms, which were installed in June 2008. These are: Platform for Intercultural Europe, Access to Culture, and Platform on the Potential of Cultural and Creative Industries.

Under its former name 'Rainbow Platform' (2006–2008), the Platform for Intercultural Europe published the 'Rainbow Paper' that includes five sets of recommendations for a well-functioning intercultural dialogue within Europe.

> Education is the first and foremost place to encourage and practice Intercultural Dialogue. Formal, non-formal and informal education can contribute to Intercultural Dialogue. Intercultural learning should be promoted in every age group and across the spectrum of educational provision. (Platform for Intercultural Europe 2008: 9)

In 2009, the platform Access to Culture produced recommendations, including a chapter dedicated to 'Education and Learning', acknowledging the role of the education sector in providing access to culture. The importance of collaboration between formal, non-formal and informal education and the contribution of arts education to the knowledge economy and lifelong learning were also emphasized.

Likewise the Platform on the Potential of Culture and Creative Industries included recommendations to stimulate education and training to bridge the gap between professional training and professional practice, to promote entrepreneurship also by including arts education in the general education and to provide opportunities for continuing professional development. (Platform on the Potential of Cultural and Creative Industries 2009: 11).

At the EU member states level, four OMC[6] groups were installed in the first phase (2007–2011), one of which focused on 'Developing synergies with education, especially arts'. The final report, which was published in June 2010 and is available online,[7] mainly focuses on formal education in school, and argues among other things for the establishment of synergies between schools, cultural institutions and artists.

Although the OMC working groups no longer operate in this way, civil servants from all members states working in the fields of arts and education continue to meet in the European Network of Civil Servants (ACEnet — Arts and Cultural Education Network).

As its contribution to the 2009 EU Year of Creativity and Innovation, the EU published a study carried out by the Eurydice network on 'Arts and Cultural Education at School in Europe' (Eurydice, 2009). The study gives an overview of arts education policies in place in 30 European countries.

The European Union has taken up the issue of arts education especially through the European Agenda for Culture and the inclusion of creativity in the strategic framework for education and training (ET 2020). However, there is still no specific programme to support arts education initiatives and with the lack of the word 'culture' in the Europe 2020 strategy it is important to continue emphasizing the importance of arts and culture and education for the European project—particularly in times of a European financial and economic crisis.

European Music Council

The European Music Council (EMC) is a non-profit organization dedicated to the development and promotion of all kinds of music in Europe. It is a network for representatives of national music councils and European music networks, as well as organizations involved in the fields of music education, creation, performance and heritage. It was founded in 1972 as the European regional group of the International Music Council (IMC), an organization created by UNESCO in 1949 to advise it on matters of music. Currently the EMC has 76 members in 29 European countries.[8] The EMC acknowledges the significant role that music and culture play in the development of a peaceful and integrated Europe. Its policies mirror those of the IMC in advocating access to music for all and promoting the Five Music Rights defined by the IMC[9]:

The right for all children and adults
- to express themselves musically in full freedom
- to learn musical languages and skills
- to have access to musical involvement through participation, listening, creation and information

The right for musical artists
- to develop their artistry and communicate through all media, with appropriate facilities at their disposal
- to obtain fair recognition and remuneration for their work

The EMC and music education

The majority of the EMC's members engage in music education, whether in formal, non-formal or informal contexts, on local, national or European level. National music councils are concerned with the situation of music education in their respective countries and work to secure adequate frameworks for music education at national level. For instance, the German Music Council has published a series of political recommendations to local and national authorities focusing on pre-school music education, music education in the *Ganztagsschulen* (schools which provide all-day education), professional training for music teachers, as well as a general position paper on the social relevance of music education in the *Erster Berliner Appell* (First Berlin Appeal) (2003)[10]. Another impressive example of lobbying is the initiative of the Swiss Music Council for a referendum to be called on the inclusion of music education in the Swiss federal constitution. The referendum will take place on 23 September 2012.

The EMC also counts many significant European and international music education networks amongst its members, such as European Association for Music in Schools (EAS), European Association of Conservatoires (AEC), European Modern Music Education Network (EMMEN), European Music School Union (EMU), European String Teachers Association (ESTA), International Society for Music Education

(ISME) and International Association of Schools of Jazz (IASJ). Furthermore, other network members, such as Jeunesses Musicales International (JMI), European Choral Association (Europa Cantat), European Federation of National Youth Orchestras (EFNYO), and European Union of Music Competitions for Youth (EMCY) have a strong educational focus in their activities.

European Forum for Music Education and Training — EFMET

In 2004 the EMC co-ordinated this EU funded project which brought together European organizations active in formal and non-formal types of music education.

The objectives of EFMET were:

- to improve European co-operation and communication between organizations active in formal and non-formal types of music education through a number of collaborative workshops and discussion rounds
- to collect information on music teacher training programmes for classroom music teachers and instrumental/vocal teachers in Europe
- to formulate recommendations for the European Commission on the place and role of (music) education and training in the new EU programme for culture after 2006[11]

Research conducted under the auspices of the EFMET project by the European Association of Conservatoires (AEC) brought together information on music teacher training programmes in 30 European countries. In the research conducted, a distinction was made between music teachers in general education and instrumental/vocal teachers teaching in music schools and private practices. Information was also compiled on the recognition of qualifications and on regulated professions in the field of music: in most European countries, music teaching in general education is a regulated profession, which poses special requirements on the mobility of musicians throughout the EU. The collection of information has been carried on by the AEC in its 'Bologna and Music' projects. The data is constantly updated and is available online at www.bologna-and-music.org.

The outcomes of EFMET show that education, training and culture are closely interlinked and that a strict separation between education, training and culture does not reflect the reality of the music sector. The project also made clear that alliances between the formal and non-formal music education sectors should be maintained and created in order to reflect the reality of the lifelong learning process and the portfolio career of the musician.

The Bonn Declaration for music education in Europe

Following its EFMET project, the EMC has continued to include music education in the agenda of its meetings and conferences. Representatives of the EMC participated in the two UNESCO World Conferences on Arts Education in Lisbon and Seoul and in 2010 the EMC launched a working group on music education that resulted in the preparation of a seminar in Bonn in May 2011. At this seminar 'From Seoul to Bonn — Translating the Goals for the Development of Arts Education for Music in

Europe' participants[12] explored the implementation of the Seoul Agenda and sought ways of adapting the document for the music sector in Europe. The outcomes of these discussions are reflected in the Bonn Declaration, a document that is directed at the music education sector and at political decision makers. It offers a matrix that music education institutions and practitioners may apply to their environments to check whether the Bonn Declaration is applicable. Furthermore, it calls upon political decision makers to implement policies that support and sustain an environment that is supportive of music education.

The Bonn Declaration reflects the three closely interlinked goals of the Seoul Agenda covering important aspects of music education, providing interpretations of these and placing its own emphasis on music education in Europe.

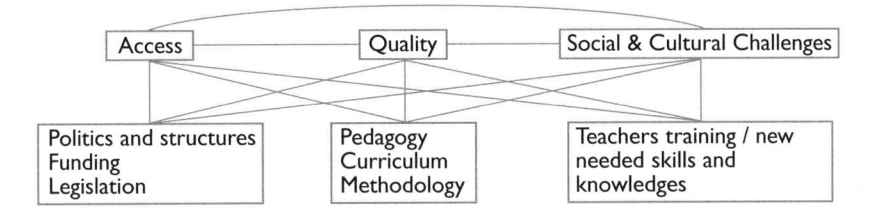

```
┌─────────┐      ┌─────────┐      ┌──────────────────────────┐
│ Access  │──────│ Quality │──────│ Social & Cultural Challenges │
└─────────┘      └─────────┘      └──────────────────────────┘

┌──────────────────────┐  ┌────────────┐  ┌──────────────────────┐
│ Politics and structures │  │ Pedagogy   │  │ Teachers training / new │
│ Funding              │  │ Curriculum │  │ needed skills and    │
│ Legislation          │  │ Methodology│  │ knowledges           │
└──────────────────────┘  └────────────┘  └──────────────────────┘
```

The interlinkage of the goals for the development of arts education and its reciprocity

The first goal of the Bonn Declaration reflects the Seoul Agenda by focusing on access: 'Access to music education and active music participation is a human right which has to be ensured for people of all ages and all backgrounds in Europe' (EMC, 2011: 2). This is in accordance with the five musical rights of the IMC referred to earlier. Themes raised in the document with regard to access to music education include lifelong learning, participatory music education as part of the curriculum, recognition of non-formal and informal music education opportunities, variation in the places in which music education is offered to reflect the diversity of society, and co-operation with other art forms and non artistic disciplines.

The second goal explores the prerequisites of high quality music education and examines 'how training institutions for educators and educators themselves meet these quality demands' (EMC, 2011: 3). In order to achieve a high quality of music education the Bonn Declaration recommends for instance the employment of high quality music education practitioners at the earliest stages of education (pre-kindergarten and pre-school education), the integration of pedagogical training in the professional training of musicians and musical training for all education professionals, as well as the development of appropriate evaluation systems (for all educational settings) and co-operation and partnerships between the diverse educational settings.

Social and cultural challenges faced by the music education sector are addressed in the third goal of the Bonn Declaration, which 're-emphasizes the potential of music for social responsibility and intercultural dialogue' (EMC, 2011: 4). For music education to meet these challenges, the Bonn Declaration states that music education should reflect the context in which it takes place, intercultural training should be included in professional training for all musicians and music education practitioners, the goals of music education projects should be defined, co-operation between formal and non-formal music education settings should be enhanced, and up-to-date facilities be available.

The Bonn Declaration concludes with a set of recommendations to political decision makers at local, national and European level. An important element of these recommendations is to secure public funding for formal, non-formal and informal music education and to ensure that music education is accessible and affordable for all. It calls for sustainable public funding that offers a balance between long-term structural funding and short-term project funding. At the same time, the recommendations ask for policies that support and sustain participatory music education, a diversity of learning (at grass-roots as well as professional level) and continuous professional training.

During the seminar in Bonn, the discussions among the participants revealed a diverse picture of music education throughout Europe. Some countries give a high level of recognition to the non-formal education setting whereas others have a very strong formal music education system that includes pedagogy as a compulsory element in the training of professional musicians. However, one commonality was striking: although official policies support music education, it is frequently the 'icing on the cake', the first area to be cut. Therefore, the Bonn Declaration includes the statement that 'political decision makers need to support and *sustain*' (my italics) its recommendations (EMC, 2011:5) — to remind them that it is not necessarily about re-inventing the wheel but also about applying the existing policies and taking them seriously.

The Bonn Declaration, published in December 2011, has already been taken up by various music education networks. For example, it provided the Greek Association of Primary Music Education Teachers with arguments for keeping music education as part of the curriculum in the primary schools in Greece. The European Music School Union has adapted it to the specifics of music schools and the European Choral Association — Europa Cantat — has been inspired to reflect the application of the three goals in the choral world.

The Bonn Declaration is a two-way document. On the one side it is directed at music education institutions and music education practitioners, offering them a matrix for self-reflection, reviewing the goals and checking whether they are applicable. On the other, it is directed towards political decision makers, and the EMC is working on disseminating the document widely to guarantee that music education is included not only in written policy documents but also in actions. With the Bonn Declaration, the EMC hopes to contribute to the implementation of the Seoul Agenda in Europe. Music education contributes to personal development and it has the power to bring people together and to contribute to peaceful and inclusive societies.

References

Access to Culture Platform (2009) *Policy Guidelines*, Brussels: July 2009.

Delors, Jacques et al. (1996) *Learning: The treasure within.* Paris, UNESCO.

European Commission (2007) *Communication from the Commission to the European Parliament, the Council, the European Economic and Social Committee and the Committee of the Regions on a European agenda for culture in a globalizing world.* Brussels: May 2007, COM 2007, 242.

European Commission (2010) *Commission report to the European Parliament, the Council, the European Economic and Social Committee and the Committee of the Regions on the implementation of the European Agenda for Culture.* Brussels: July 2010, COM (2010)390 final.

EMC (2011) *The Bonn Declaration for Music Education in Europe.* Bonn: European Music Council.

European Union (2009) *Council conclusions of 12 May 2009 on a strategic framework for European co-operation in education and training ('ET 2020').* Brussels: Official Journal of the European Union (2009/C 119/02).

Eurydice (2009) *Arts and Cultural Education at School in Europe.* Brussels: Education, Audiovisual and Culture Executive Agency.

O'Farrell, Larry (2010) *Final Report. Closing Session of The Second World Conference on Arts Education Seoul.* Paris: UNESCO.

Platform for Intercultural Europe (2008) *The Rainbow Paper. Intercultural Dialogue: From Practice to Policy and Back.* Brussels: Platform for Intercultural Europe.

Platform on Access to Cutlure (2009) *Policy Guidelines.* Brussels, Platform on Access to Culture.

Platform on the Potential of Cultural and Creative Industries (2009). *Recommendations for Cultural and Creative Industries.* Brussels: Platform on the Potential of Cultural and Creative Industries.

UNESCO (1948) *Records of the General Conference of the United Nations Educational, Scientific and Cultural Organization.* Paris: UNESCO.

UNESCO (1999) *Records of the General Conference, 30th Session Paris, 26 October to 17 November 1999.* Paris: UNESCO.

UNESCO (2005) *Convention on the Protection and Promotion of the Diversity of Cultural Expressions.* Paris: UNESCO.

UNESCO (2006) *Road Map for Arts Education. Building Creative Capacities for the 21st Century.* Paris: UNESCO.

UNESCO (2010) *The Second World Conference on Arts Education. Seoul Agenda: Goals for the Development of Arts Eduation.* Paris: UNESCO.

Websites

International Drama/Theatre and Education Association (IDEA) www.idea-org.net/

International Society for Education through Art (INSEA) www.insea.org

International Society for Music Education (ISME) www.isme.org

International Network for Research in Arts Education (INRAE): www.arts-edu.org

UNESCO Arts Education Portal EU culture portal http://ec.europa.eu/culture

EU education portal http://ec.europa.eu/education/index_en.htm

UNESCO Chair Arts & Learning http://educ.queensu.ca/unesco/arts-and-learning.html

UNESCO Chair in Arts and Culture in Education www.paedagogik.phil.uni-erlangen.de/institut/

Further reading

Bamford, Anne (2006) *The Wow Factor. Global research compendium on the impact of the arts in education.* Münster: Waxman.

Bamford, Anne (2010) 'Setting the Agenda for Cultural Change for the 21st Century'. *Sounds in Europe #6*: 20–22. Bonn: European Music Council.

Deutscher Musikrat *Musik bewegt. Positionspapiere zur Musikalischen Bildung.* Berlin: Deutscher Musikrat.

EMC (European Music Council) (2004) *EFMET European Forum for Music Education and Training. Recommendations to the European Union about the role of music education and training in the new EU programme for culture.* Bonn: European Music Council.

Liebau, Eckart & Wagner, Ernst (2011) *UNESCO und die kulturelle Bildung.* Bonn: Bundeszentrale für politische Bildung.

O'Farrell, Larry (2011) *The Seoul Agenda: Goals, Strategies and Action Items.* Presentation in the frame of the 3rd IMC World Forum on Music. www.worldforumonmusic.org/ fileadmin/ IMC-WFM/sessions/OFarrell.pdf.

Wimmer, Michael (2006) *Promoting Cultural Educaiton in Europe. A Contribution to Participation, Innovation and Quality.* Vienna: Austrian Ministry of Education, Science and Culture.

Wimmer, Michael (2011) *Von den Rändern ins Zentrum: Kulturelle Bildung in Europa.* Online-Dossier. Bonn: Bundeszentrale für Politische Bildung.

Endnotes

[1] www.unesco.org/new/en/culture/themes/creativity/arts-education/about/background/

[2] Both quotations from www.unesco.org/new/en/culture/themes/creativity/arts-education/about/ approach/ accessed July 2012

[3] http://europa.eu/legislation_summaries/culture/index_en.htm, accessed July 2012

[4] http://europa.eu/legislation_summaries/education_training_youth/general_framework/ index_en.htm, accessed July 2010

[5] The Lisbon strategy is considered to have failed, the succeeding EU strategy is 'Europe 2020' with the aim of smart, sustainable and inclusive growth for the European economy. Education is one of the key pillars to reach this aim, whereas culture is not mentioned in the strategy at all.

[6] The Open Method of Coordination (OMC), provides a new framework for co-operation between the EU Member States, whose national policies can thus be directed towards certain common objectives. The open method of coordination takes place in areas which fall within the competence of the Member States. See: http://europa.eu/legislation_summaries/glossary/ open_method_coordination_en.htm.

The Culture Council introduced a first work plan to implement the European Agenda in 2007. In the first phase (2007–2011) the following OMC groups were installed:
- Working group on mobility of culture professionals
- Working group on cultural and creative industries
- Working Group on Synergies between culture and education, especially arts education
- Working group on museum activities

In the second phase (2011–2014) the following OMC groups have started working on:
- cultural diversity and dialogue/accessible and inclusive culture
- cultural and creative industries
- skills and mobility
- cultural heritage (including mobility of collections).

7   http://ec.europa.eu/culture/key-documents/doc/MOCedu_final_report_en.pdf
8   Cf www.emc-imc.org/about
9   www.imc-cim.org/about-imc-separator/five-music-rights.html
10 www.musikrat.de/no_cache/musikpolitik/musikalische-bildung/1-berliner-appell.html?sword_list%5B%5D=appell
11 www.emc-imc.org/?id=257
12 Over 40 representatives of European music education networks were present, representing formal, non-formal and informal music education and different genres.

Appendix

Useful websites and further reading

Funded opportunities for professional exchange, collaboration, volunteering and research

British Council: Lifelong Learning Programme (LLP) This provides opportunities for organizations, staff and learners involved in education and training across Europe to work together, learn from each others' expertise, and widen their experience of other cultures and languages. Funded by the European Commission, the LLP supports a wide range of education and training activities across Europe and provides opportunities for all stages of lifelong learning. In the UK thousands of projects are funded each year. The LLP is made up of several programmes, each aimed at a specific target group:

- Schools: **Comenius and eTwinning**
- Higher Education: **Erasmus**
- Vocational Education and Training: **Leonardo**
- Adult Education (non vocational): **Grundtvig**
- Learning professionals: **Transversal**

www.britishcouncil.org

British Council: International School Award (ISA) The British Council offers this as an accreditation framework for schools to record and evaluate their international work and embed it into the curriculum and whole school ethos, There is at least one music focused project listed. 'International Voices' develops partnerships between schools in the UK and around the world, with music and singing at the heart of the project. http://schoolsonline.britishcouncil.org/International-School-Award

The Commonwealth Teacher Exchange was initiated by the League for the Exchange of Commonwealth Teachers (LECT). It is officially recognized by the UK Government for allocation of Tier 5 visas to enable exchange counterparts to work in UK, and similar arrangements exist for UK teachers to obtain visas to work in Canada and Australia on a post-to-post exchange basis. www.cyec.org

The Fulbright Teacher Exchange Program The Fulbright Teacher Exchange Program seeks to improve mutual understanding among teachers, their schools and communities in the U.S. and abroad through two programmes — the Fulbright Classroom Teacher Exchange Program and the Distinguished Fulbright Awards in Teaching Program. www.fulbrightteacherexchange.org/

VSO works in education in 17 countries. VSO education volunteers are part of a global effort to make sure every child can access quality primary education by 2015. www.vso.org.uk/volunteer/opportunities/teaching-and-education/index.asp

Winston Churchill Memorial Trust awards Travelling Fellowships to British citizens from all walks of life to travel overseas, to bring back knowledge and best practice for the benefit of others in their UK professions and communities. Categories change each year and deadline is October. www.wcmt.org.uk/

Organizations promoting international networking for music educators

The **European Association for Music in Schools (EAS)** provides a network for all music educators concerned with general music education. EAS holds a conference in a different location each year across Europe (2013 Belgium; 2014 Cyprus). Alongside a programme of presentations and workshops, it provides forums for debate and for student teachers, doctoral students, and national association representatives to work together. It partners with ISME to hold the ISME regional conference. www.eas-music.org

The **European Association of Conservatoires** is a European cultural and educational network with 280 member institutions for professional music training in 55 countries. www.aecinfo.org

The **European Music Council** is a Regional Group of the International Music Council. www.emc-imc.org

The **European Music School Union** is the European umbrella organization of national music school associations in Europe. The EMU represents a supranational platform comprised of member associations from various countries. www.musicschoolunion.eu

The **International Society for Music Education (ISME)** holds a biennial world conference for practitioners and researchers—there are opportunities to bring performance groups and cultural visits and music of the host country are always included. The next two conferences are in Brazil (2014) and Glasgow (2016). www.isme.org

The **International Music Council (IMC)**, founded in 1949 by UNESCO, is the world's largest network of organizations, institutions and individuals working in the field of music. The International Music Council promotes musical diversity, access to culture for all and unites organizations in some 150 countries worldwide in building peace and understanding among peoples of all cultures and heritage. They hold a World Forum on Music every two years—the next will be 2013. www.imc-cim.org

Information, commentaries and research in the international field of education and music education

meNet is a Comenius-3 network funded by the European Commission's Programme Sokrates-Comenius. 26 institutions from 11 countries participated. *meNet* collects, compiles and disseminates knowledge about music education in schools and music teacher training in Europe. Project duration: October 2006–September 2009. Results can be found at www.menet.info. Ongoing work is carried out by EAS.

The **Eurydice Network** provides information on and analysis of European education systems and policies. As from 2012 it consists of 38 national units based in all 34 countries participating in the EU's Lifelong Learning programme (EU Member States, EFTA countries, Croatia, Serbia and Turkey). It is co-ordinated and managed by the EU Education, Audiovisual and Culture Executive Agency in Brussels, which drafts its studies and provides a range of online resources. http://eacea.ec.europa.eu/education/eurydice/index_en.php

Music Education Research is an internationally refereed journal which draws its contributions from a wide community of researchers. It provides an international forum for cross-cultural investigations and discussions relating to all areas of music education. It is concerned with the dissemination of ideas relating to practical and theoretical developments in the field of music education. www.tandfonline.com/

British Journal of Music Education is a fully refereed international journal which aims to provide accounts of contemporary research in music education worldwide. The journal strives to strengthen connections between research and practice, so enhancing professional development and improving practice within the field of music education. http://journals.cambridge.org/bjme

McPherson, G. & Welch, G. (eds.) (2012) *Oxford Handbook of Music Education (2 volumes)*. Oxford: OUP.

Kertz-Welzel, A. (2008) Music Education in the 21st century: A cross-cultural comparison of German and American music education towards a new concept of global exchange. *Music Education Research*, 10(4): 439–449.

Burnard, P., Dillon, S.C., Rusinek, G. & Saether, E. (2008) Inclusive pedagogies in music education: A comparative study of music teachers' perspectives from four countries. *International Journal of Music Education*, 26(2): 109–126.

Arostegui, J.C. (ed.) (2011) *Educating Music Teachers for the 21st century*. Rotterdam: Sense Books (and Ebook available free at www.nisearch.com).